The X & Y of Leadership

The X & Y of Leadership

by
Liz Cook and Brian Rothwell

First published in 2000 by
The Industrial Society
Robert Hyde House
48 Bryanston Square
London W1H 7LN
Telephone: 020 7479 2000

© The Industrial Society, 2000

ISBN 1 85835 895 7

The Industrial Society
Business Books Network
163 Central Avenue, Suite 2
Hopkins Professional Building
Dover, NH 03820
USA

British Library Cataloguing-in-Publication Data.
A catalogue record for this book is available from the
British Library.

Library of Congress Cataloguing-in-Publication Data on
File.

Typeset by: The Midlands Book Typesetting Company
Printed by: J. W. Arrowsmiths
Cover by: Sign Design
Cover image: Tony Stone

The Industrial Society is a Registered Charity No. 290003
746 SL 5.99

Acknowledgements

To the many people who have helped and supported us both in our work and in the writing of this book – thank you! In particular, we would like to individually appreciate the following for their advice, guidance, inspiration, interest and time.

Debra Allcock-Tyler
Janice Andrew
Vicki Beeke
Alison Beeney
Tony Bolton
Cathy Bourne
Chris Bourne
Jacob Brown
Tom Carpenter
Mary Clements
Charles Collingwood
Jenny Davenport
Chris Day
Keith Evans
Nigel Ewington
Paul Gidley
Judith Harding
Jonathan Harradine
Paula Healey
Peter Hill
Christine Ingebrigtsen
Rohini Kochar
Ian Lawson
Richard Livesey-Howarrth
Margaret Lloyd
Lisa Collette MacFarlane
Lewis Maciver
John McCusker

Brendan McDonagh
Clare Martin
Diane Mather
Marje Mills
Tony Morgan
Amelia Jane Milligan
Jane Milligan
Peter Nathan
Sue Newell
Ray Noyes
Lesley O'Dell
Steve O'Smotherly
Richard Olivier
Jacqui Pattison
Ann Paul
Colin Pugsley
Maggie Rose
Sue Rothwell
Bob Satchwell
Vijay Sharma
Alice Sorby
Carole Taylor
Rob Taylor
Alison Tickner
Carl Upsall
John Walkley
Miki Walleczek
Anne Watson Jones

Contents

Foreword

'Somewhere downtown in the busy world,
Amongst the siren-haunted high-rise,
There is a place or a time where something
Tremendous is waiting to happen.
In a moment the over-carpeted world can change;
Swing wide, to reveal a hidden landscape
Of unimaginable promise – right there
Among the plans and the projected targets'

WILLIAM AYOT

The call to the future is a call to appropriate leadership. Whether we lead a multinational company, a private business, a community or simply our own lives, there is a growing need to understand the different styles and attributes that will inform the leader of the future. This timely book provides a valuable guide to those who seek to exploit their potential as leaders.

Human beings from all cultures have recognised that there are general differences between men and women, although every culture would not agree on what these differences are. Some of the recent and important efforts to minimise sex discrimination have tended to diminish these differences. How refreshing, therefore, to read a sensible, clear and balanced account based on recent scientific evidence that re-proposes we are 'different and equal'.

Women spent a good part of the twentieth century redefining their role in modern society, and although there are undoubtedly both overt and covert vestiges of discrimination and inequality still to overcome in the twenty-first century, there is no turning back. Skirmishes remain, but the crucial battle is won. Karl Marx's belief that only violent revolution can change the power structure and his assertion that 'no ruling class will ever give up power willingly' have happily been proved fallible.

In general it is women who have conducted this re-positioning work, while men have tried to adjust (or have resisted or adjusted begrudgingly). As individuals and as a group, men can now take stock of where they have been in order to accurately assess their current position, and – crucially for the future of the planet – where they want to go. This book explains the skills that men will require to become more responsive and co-operative.

Some of this enquiry may prove hard for men at first. It will require openness, reflection, connecting and listening skills (to name only a few), all attributes which Liz and Brian convincingly show as characteristic of the typical feminine brain. But we would do well to remember that women were only able to achieve their breakthroughs by examining and occasionally adopting certain traits that appear typically masculine, including focus, challenging the status quo, inventiveness and action orientation.

This book will help women to realise that, while they may learn from masculine leadership styles, they do not have to act like men in order to work as equals, and men should recognise that learning a more typically feminine skill set will not reduce their leadership effectiveness, but rather enhance it.

The distinctions made in this book will help both men and women understand each other better, and appreciate how the other gender may wish to lead and be led. When that happens we may well find 'a hidden landscape of unimaginable promise'.

Richard Olivier
Creative Consultant, Group Facilitator

Introduction

The differences that divide and unite the authors

The authors are divided by their biology. One inherited a 23rd chromosome from her father that was shaped like an X. The other was bequeathed a Y chromosome. They also differ in other ways.

Brian Rothwell is a self-employed entrepreneur with interests in four different and risk-taking businesses. Liz Cook is a management consultant who has worked for the same organisation for the last 12 years, but with different responsibilities.

Liz's *domestic* telephone bill typically runs at £250 per quarter. She spends, on average, four nights a week at home in between business trips to visit clients. Brian's *business* telephone bill, from the same supplier, typically runs at £150 per quarter. He works alone, spending, on average, six days a week on business relationships that are dependent on a telephone link.

Even under the stresses of lecturing together, when extreme concentration is needed to pick up script cues from each other, Liz can think of other things she needs to do. Brian is so single-minded and focused that his wife knows that if she wants his full attention she must turn the TV or the radio off and remove the book from his hand.

When asked to spontaneously conjure up an image that she associated with the word 'team', Liz came up with *'A group of people who supported and encouraged others at work'*. Brian's image was one of a rugby team holding a trophy after a succession of victories.

Brian solves problems by thinking them through logically on his own. Liz tackles her problems by relying on a 'gut' feeling and talking the issue through with colleagues or friends until a solution becomes apparent.

Liz can cook a risotto and mix a salad at the same time. Brian can do one followed by the other, but not both simultaneously.

They can both parallel park! Brian has been able to do this naturally since learning to drive at the age of 17. Liz has acquired this skill over many years of having to park in tight spaces outside her clients' offices.

The results of electronic imaging have shown that their brains are very different: one is typically male, while the other is averagely female. Consequently they think and act differently when faced with similar leadership situations. Nevertheless they have worked together successfully for the past two years, bringing very different skills and qualities to the partnership, and at the same time they have learned considerably from each other.

1

Setting the scene

'I am always ready to learn, although I do not always like to be taught'
WINSTON CHURCHILL

This is a book about leadership. Its purpose is to improve the relationships between men and women at work. We wish to heighten the understanding of the different ways that women and men choose to lead and decide to follow others, and to encourage both sexes to value these differences.

A rapidly growing body of evidence maintains that the human sexes are divided by different brain engineering. As the techniques of brain imaging continue to advance, we can now watch our own brains function. Researchers and volunteers can now literally watch, via a computer screen, as their own brains learn a new word, recall a sad incident or even laugh. The clarity of these images provides the evidence that the brains of the average woman and man differ as much their physiques.

We accept that any division of men and women into different gender categories might prove both offensive to some and misleading to others. However, we are prepared to run this risk because, in our opinion, the danger of denying or ignoring the differences is greater than the danger of labelling them.

If we ignore the real and scientifically proven differences between the brains of the sexes, and therefore in the way they think and act, we risk increasing the confusion that exists in this age of constantly changing relationships between men and women at work. If the sexes think and act differently when exposed to similar stimuli, we believe that it logically follows that they will think and act differently when leading others. In saying this, we recognise that we are likely to start many discussions, and even arguments, but we do hope to add information to the debate.

We welcome opposing views, and encourage those who wish to express them to contact The Industrial Society via the mail, fax, Email or website addresses listed at the end of this book. We guarantee that everyone will receive a reply.

This book is not intended to provide a definitive answer. New facts and theories are emerging as we write. We live in times of exponentially increasing change in which all knowledge is temporary and when any leadership theory, or model, will inevitably have a short life.

The importance of leadership today

We believe passionately in the concept of leadership and the part it has to play in moulding the future of our society. At the start of the twenty-first century, tensions and contradictions are growing within our society. There is a widespread rejection of the values and priorities of business leaders, mistrust of the motives of politicians and a growing demand for higher ethical standards.

We have more access to knowledge and information than ever before and yet we struggle to manage this plethora of facts and figures. People are demanding a higher quality of life and yet stress is at unprecedented levels. The state is gradually withdrawing from welfare support. As individuals we are expected to be accountable for our own actions and to take responsibility for our own lives. At the same time we are becoming more responsible for the wider community, as individuals, employers and voluntary organisations strive to fill the gap left by the state. These are all leadership issues.

The leadership skills and strategies needed to steer us through these contradictions and tensions are derived both from processes and the quality of relationships that we develop and nurture with other people. In order to sustain a competitive, healthy economy and society, we need to develop leadership that is based on ethical outcomes, shared values and mutual trust.

We make a fundamental distinction between management and leadership. Leadership is the people aspect of management. Management is fundamentally about non-human resources or things. One manages things and one leads people. Management is a science taught as a university degree subject, whereas leadership can be termed an art. Warren Bennis characterises management as being about doing things right; whereas leadership is about doing the right things.

Our stance on the equality issue

This is a book about leadership, not about the existence of sex equality or inequality in the workplace. We believe that both sexes bring considerable, but different, strengths to the leadership role. We also believe that both sexes can learn leadership behaviours, attributes and competencies from each other and that this learning experience can benefit the working and personal lives of both leaders and followers.

Our contention is that the sexes are different and, on average, men and women choose to lead and follow others in different ways. This point has nothing to do with equality. Equality is an ethical, moral, political and social concept that we both support wholeheartedly. In contrast, the biological and statistical differences between the sexes that we describe later in this book are scientific facts. We believe that the sexes can be different and equal as leaders.

Difference is not the opposite of equality. Equality means being free to choose the things we want to do and the ways we want to behave as leaders. In contrast, difference means that, as men or as women, we are not naturally inclined to do the same things or behave in the same way when leading others.

We hope that in discussing the facts and issues surrounding the different natural abilities that women and men bring to leadership, others will not exploit the opportunity to devalue the need to campaign for equal pay and value for both men and women at work. Our belief is that our natural abilities should bring the same reward for the same effort. It is not our intention to divert attention from the issue of continuing sex discrimination in some organisations, neither is it our intention to hand back the 'power base' to men or to acquire it for women.

We accept that women in the UK today do not currently enjoy equality at work with their male colleagues. Despite the equality legislation and cultural changes of the last three decades, there is still an imbalance between the sexes at work that needs rectifying. Although some progress has been made, most women still report to male bosses. Ninety percent of the top leadership jobs in the UK are still held by men. This statistic has changed little during the last thirty years.

'Women's work', particularly in the teaching and caring sectors of the economy, is still undervalued when compared to other more male-dominated occupations. Average wealth and income remains much lower for women than for men.

Although girls continue to outperform boys academically at secondary school and males dominate the categories of the homeless, the down-and-outs and the street dwellers, there are very few other indications that men are the new oppressed sex. Male dominance at work continues to exist and is in need of some forms of societal and cultural correction.

We stand for women and men having an equal opportunity to pursue the career of their choice. We also maintain that equally gifted, qualified and experienced people should receive equal employment terms and conditions for the input of the same effort.

We also believe that it is vital that leaders know 'why they are the way they are'. Self-knowledge is vital to effective performance as a leader. We therefore wish to ignore the equality imperfections within the current UK working environment and concentrate on what it could become if leaders had a better understanding of themselves. The differences between the sexes are part of this vital understanding.

There is a leadership crisis within British society today. We are not tapping the well of the capacities of all of our male and female workers, colleagues and citizens. We need the initiative of everyone, irrespective of their sex, at whatever level they work, in order to remain a healthy and competitive economy within a compassionate society.

Understanding the differences in the ways that women and men choose to lead and follow is an important part of this improvement process. We believe men and women should be equal in their rights to develop their full potential as human beings. However, we also stand for the fact that women and men, on average, are not identical in their innate leadership abilities.

During the two years that it has taken us to research and write this book, one point of view became increasingly obvious to us. Educated females in leadership positions were far more likely to have read at least some of the works we refer to than their male equivalents; and having done so were far more likely to appreciate the leadership differences we have identified. Quite often these females thought they had nothing to learn from male leaders and that it was men who needed to change. This is not a view we endorse. Our view is that men and women have much to learn from each other in the context of leadership.

We do not wish to stereotype either sex

We stand for leaders engaging with others as people, not as stereotypical men or women. We need leaders who can think as others do and connect with minds other than their own. We need female leaders who can think like men and male leaders who can think like women.

Every one of us, whether female or male, is shaped by innumerable influences, including parental values, religion, race, class, profession, age, education, area of upbringing as well as the genes we inherited; and these are all mixed up with our own individual personality and preferences.

Leaders of both sexes may read this book and exclaim, *'This does not fit with my behaviour'* or *'I don't think like that'*. This is a perfectly valid response. We do not presume that every leader of the male sex will automatically think, act and behave in a masculine way or that every leader of the female sex will automatically think, act and behave in a feminine way. Neither do we presume that every leader of each sex should think, act or behave in a particular way. We accept that every human being is unique.

However, we defend our right to generalise across the sexes. For example, it is a true and fair generalisation to say that men are taller than women. The average man is taller than the average woman. It is also true to say that the tallest woman in most groups of human beings will be taller than the shortest man. All men are therefore not taller than all women.

The same spread applies to the functioning of the average male and the average female brain. The average woman has more rods in her brain than the average man and is, therefore, better at some aspects of seeing in the dark than the average man. It is also true that there will be many women who can see less well in the dark than the man with the best night vision. All women, therefore, are not better at seeing in the dark than all men.

We are not arguing that one sex is better than the other but simply that if one is male there is a likelihood that one will have a height advantage over a female. And that if one is female there is a likelihood that one will have a night-sight advantage over a male.

We apply the same logic to leadership capabilities and ask you to accept that there will be many individual exceptions to every feminine and masculine leadership behaviour and attribute we distinguish.

Genes and upbringing

We accept and welcome the belief that every person is a unique and unrepeatable mixture of genes and upbringing. However, in the nature versus nurture debate, we come down firmly on the side of nature, a stance that we know will cause some controversy.

Our publishers, The Industrial Society, asked readers for their comments on the first draft of this book. The following remark came from a professor of neurology: *'My profession has known of the differences between male and female brains for two generations – why on earth would you want to feature these differences in a book today?'* The implication here is that the view we express is old news. We agree that neurologists have known most of the facts we quote for a long time, but maintain that these facts have not been easily accessible to the wider public.

Another comment from a professor of psychology maintained that *'The differences between the two sexes described in the draft are exaggerated'*. The implication here is that we were treading on dangerous ground in highlighting the differences between masculine and feminine leadership thinking and action. This reaction, in our opinion, is a reflection of a 'politically correct' attitude that attributes any differences in the sexes solely, or mainly, to upbringing and social factors.

We agree that nurture has its part to play and we also agree that naturally men and women are different. Our position, as non-academics, is that nature and nurture work in the same direction. Nurture reinforces nature and enhances the biological differences that emerge from the average male and female brain. The research indicates that the average male child reaches naturally for the toy tractor and is encouraged to do so by most parents, most of his relations and most of society as a whole. In a similar way the average female child reaches naturally for the toy doll and is again encouraged to do so by most of the members of society with whom she is in contact.

Further, our main emphasis is not to devalue or argue about the influence of nature or nurture. We believe that a leadership attribute, whether acquired by nature or nurture, can be developed or changed by learning and practice. We wish to build on the attributes displayed by both sexes to improve the leadership capabilities of all leaders irrespective of their sex.

The terminology we use

Male and female

All human societies consist of men and women and usually they live together in approximately equal numbers. The two sexes have absolutely different roles in the procreation of offspring.

Other biological differences between the sexes are not absolute; they are statistical. For example, women have, on average, greater finger dexterity and recover faster from fatigue than men, but some men also excel at these attributes. These differences, which are similar the world over, are statistical rather than absolute.

Differences in the brains of the average male and the average female are also statistical rather than absolute. It is estimated that 80–85% of males have male-engineered brains and about 15–20% have brains that have been feminised to a lesser or greater extent. It is estimated that 10% of women have brains that have been masculinised to a certain extent.

When we refer to these biological absolute and statistical differences between the sexes we will use the terms male and female, or man and woman.

Masculine and feminine

The social roles adopted by the two sexes are only partially determined by the procreation process. Every society recognises many thinking patterns and behaviours, unrelated to procreation, as more feminine or more masculine. But which thinking patterns and behaviours belong to which gender differs from one society to another.

Anthropologists who have studied non-literate and relatively isolated societies stress the wide variety of social sex roles that are possible. In some societies women do most of the agricultural work and in others barely none. In some societies men make pots or weave cloth, in others they do not.

Likewise, in modern societies there are more female than male medical doctors in Russia and more female than male dentists in Belgium. In the UK men statistically dominate these jobs. Men form the majority of typists in Pakistan and constitute a large part of the nursing profession in the Netherlands, again in contrast to the UK. Female managers are virtually non-existent in Japan but women manage all the shops in parts of West Africa. This reflects different cultures, customs and practices.

The societal context against which any gender generalisation is made varies enormously across both ancient and modern societies. However, in spite of the variety that exists, the gender roles of masculinity and femininity do show some common threads across different societies.

Masculine roles are commonly associated with success outside the home: hunting or ploughing in earlier civilisations and their equivalents in more modern societies. Masculinity is associated with independence, action, competitiveness and toughness. Femininity is associated with taking care of the home and the children, and of people in general. In contrast with independence and toughness, femininity is associated with relationship-building and tenderness.

Hofstede, in particular, has used the concepts of masculinity and femininity to define national cultures. In feminine cultures the dominant values are caring for others and preservation. People work in order to live. Norway, Sweden, Denmark and the Netherlands top the table for femininity. In masculine cultures the dominant values are material success and progress. People live in order to work. Japan tops this table for masculinity with the USA following closely behind.

In leadership terms masculine and feminine cultures create different role models. The masculine leader is assertive and decisive. He, or she, is a lonely decision-maker who looks for facts discretely rather than engaging others in dialogue to find a solution to a problem. The leader in a feminine culture is less visible, intuitive rather than decisive, and is accustomed to seeking the views of others.

The UK is defined as a relatively masculine culture, featuring joint ninth in Hofstede's list of more than 50 countries. We write as individuals who have only experienced work in the UK culture. One invisible backdrop to this book is therefore a masculine work culture, and our comments are not transferable to other very different national cultures. A second invisible influence is the fact that we are both white and of Anglo-Saxon descent. We are not representative of men and women in the UK generally. We do not presume to talk for any ethnic-minority grouping resident in the UK, amongst whom the leadership relationships between the sexes at work may be very different.

Individual leaders are also greatly influenced by the culture of the organisation within which they work. Each organisation has a leadership culture that can be described as either feminine or masculine (Appendix 2). We accept the point that there are many more women in the UK who operate within a culture which is still predominantly masculine than vice versa. Leaders operate within the constraints and confines of their own organisational culture.

Our belief is that when men are gathered together a masculine leadership culture is likely to predominate and where women prevail a feminine leadership culture will be the norm. The feminine leadership culture is likely to be foreign to most men and a masculine culture alien to most women. Exposure to an organisational culture different to the one we are used to is likely to cause a 'culture shock'. Despite this 'shock' we believe individual women can learn to function effectively as leaders in a masculine culture and individual men can learn to function just as effectively in a feminine culture.

When we refer to socially or culturally determined roles, or to the leadership attributes that stem from the different brains of males and females, we will use the terms masculine and feminine. These terms are relative, not absolute. A man can act in a relatively feminine way and a woman in a relatively masculine way. This relativity reflects only that the sexes can deviate from certain conventions in their own society. We wish to cause no offence to masculine women or feminine men in any societal context.

Let us restate our purpose, which is to improve the relationships between the sexes at work. We do not wish to denigrate or stereotype either sex. Our objective is to enable leaders of either sex to encourage everyone to fulfil their potential at work.

References

Bennis, W. & Goldsmith, J., *Learning to Lead*, Nicholas Brealey, 1997.

Greenfield, S., *The Human Brain: A Guided Tour*, Phoenix, 1997.

Hofstede, G., *Culture's Consequences*, Sage Publications, 1980.

Lawson, I., *Leaders for Tomorrow's Society*, The Industrial Society, 1999.

Pease, A. & B., *Why Men Don't Listen & Women Can't Read Maps*, PTI, 1999.

Tannen, D., *You Just Don't Understand: Men & Women in Conversation*, Virago Press, 1992.

Wajcman, J., *Managing Like a Man*, Polity, 1999.

2

The path we have taken

'Life does not consist mainly – or even largely – of facts and happenings. It consists mainly of a storm of thoughts that is forever blowing through one's head'

MARK TWAIN

Our starting point

We, the authors, first met on a leadership conference in 1997. At this conference one of the speakers *dared* to imply that science could now prove that males and females possessed different ways of thinking and behaving. What he started to say was that, in social interaction, men tend to occupy more physical space than women – in the pub and on the commuter train – and that this is not just a function of a bigger average physical frame.

They tend to spread their arms and legs more, and are more likely to surround themselves with the status symbols of power, such as the briefcase, the mobile phone and the laptop computer. Men also tend to boast of their achievements more than women do. Men talk of what they have done or what they have achieved. They sometimes even boast of how ill they have been, of how they can cope and work even with a temperature of 105!

The speaker got no further. At this point, several female managers from the audience challenged his right to imply that the sexes were different. Even though he had talked only about males, he had offended their perception of equality.

This incident formed the basis of the discussion of our first lunch meeting. We agreed that the female managers with feminist tendencies were probably denying a difference between the sexes that should be self-evident. We had a sneaking feeling that the thinking and acting patterns of males and females were indeed different, but we didn't know how to prove it.

We had both grown up in the white, Anglo-Saxon, middle-class world of office work in England. And over more than two decades both of us had been brought up to believe that the sexes were equal. This mindset had led us, and we believe many others, to assume that the sexes were the same – that they shared the same thinking patterns and would react in the same way to a given stimulus.

We had the intriguing notion that something was missing from the debate, and yet we could not quite put our fingers on it. We are both full-time working managers and had, at the time, never read or seen a book or an article describing the differences in the brains of the human sexes.

The daily lives of most individuals are full of things that keep us busy and preoccupied. Every now and again we may draw back and ask ourselves fundamental philosophical questions. The question we started with was *'What do we mean by equality?'* In so doing, we were questioning a fundamental issue that we had both always taken for granted.

Today, equal opportunity is the rule of law. The Equal Pay Act had, after all, been passed in 1970, the first Sex Discrimination Act in 1975 and the EEC Directive on Equal Treatment in the same year. For nearly three decades equality has been the cry in the world of the employed in the UK. And with this cry for equality has come the 'politically correct' notion that the sexes were the same. This, with hindsight, was the mindset we intended to challenge.

The lunch conversation that day led us to open our thinking that perhaps the mindset of sameness could be challenged. We agreed that all of our experiences are lodged in the databank of our subconscious. Brian can remember his words: *'If a male has created a subconscious databank that has experienced all things and emotions through a male brain, logically his thoughts should emerge as male thoughts. My subconscious thoughts emerge while driving down motorways when my brain is in neutral. They also emerge through dreams. In my dreams I am always a man. What do your dreams picture you as?'* Liz agreed that in her dreams she was never male. Sometimes she was an object or an animal, but she was never a male human being.

We speculated on the fact that although water is essential for the survival of a fish, yet the fish cannot see the water. What makes us human beings is the 'water' that is automatically all around us but which we cannot see. Brian was surrounded by 'male water', Liz by 'female water'.

We all learn to do things automatically. We learned to drive and, after a time, we do it automatically. We do it so automatically that we sometimes cannot remember having driven the familiar journey home from work. A lot of learning is about forgetting. A lot of learning is about doing things automatically, so automatically that we have forgotten how we learned to do them.

We are so used to looking at the world *through* a male or a female lens that we are not used to looking *at* the lens. At that point we turned our attention to the lens of our own femaleness and maleness.

The key question that day became: *'If one is female and has only ever thought in a female way through a female brain, how can one know that there is another way to think?'* And its corollary: *'If one is male and has only ever thought in a male way through a male brain, how can one know that there is another way to think?'* And this led to: *'How does a male know that his thinking is masculine?'* and *'How does a female know that her thinking is feminine?'* We speculated further: *'Is male thinking the product of his male genes or his social upbringing?'* and *'Is female thinking the product of her female genes or her social upbringing?'*

People have always been able to get inside the heads of the opposite sex and speak, write and think in the language of the opposite gender. In novels such as *The Ice People*, female novelists like Maggie Gee have written of life through the eyes of a man. Dustin Hoffman acted the part of a woman very convincingly in the film *Tootsie*. It must be possible for a woman to think and act like a man and for a man to think and act like a woman.

At that first meeting our conversation focused on the nurture side of the nature versus nurture debate. We speculated, all too fleetingly, about the fact that there may be a natural explanation for gender difference. After all, we are not scientists: Liz is a management consultant with a preference for people rather than process, and Brian is a businessman with an economics degree.

As we left that first meeting, Liz recommended that if Brian wanted to learn to think like her, he had better go away and read *Bridget Jones's Diary* by Helen Fielding. This recounts the daily life of a thirty-something, single female from a similar sort of background to Brian – middle class, university educated, employed in an office – and yet Brian didn't understand half of the emotions and feelings she described. Why did she make so many 1471 calls? Why was she so obsessed by her weight? Why were there so many relationships in her life and why did they give her so much angst? Brian could not grasp her concept of self. To him it was like reading a book in a foreign language.

To Liz, however, Bridget Jones was reality. It made sense to her. For Brian, despite living and working with females all his life (he is married to one, the father of another and had several close female friends), he didn't know how they thought about the world. It was so different from the way that he thought about the world. It could almost be a different world. Brian concluded that perhaps there was something to be gained from learning to think like a woman.

Two days later, he received a card from Liz. A simple thank-you for lunch, it contained a quotation from Confucius: *'By nature man is nearly alike; by practice, he gets to be miles apart.'* He wasn't sure whether Liz was referring to the absence of the female gender in the words or whether she was commenting on the nurture versus nature debate. Brian was beginning to realise that there may be another way of thinking that was very different from his own.

The beginning of understanding

Our research review has taken us from university gender studies departments to psychology faculties. But it was in a biology faculty where we found a starting point. There we discovered brain-imaging computer screens involved in unravelling the mysteries of the human brain, and evidence that the average male brain differs from the average female brain. And we were by no means the only ones on this trail!

When we started this research, in 1997, very little had been written on the subject that was accessible to the lay person. Today, only two years later, there is a plethora of books and articles extolling and explaining the differences in the brains of males and females and the way in which they behave.

One book, written by Rita Carter, a medical journalist, contains pictures of the differences in male and female brains in a chapter entitled 'The sexual brain'. Another, written by psychologist Elizabeth Mapstone, is entitled *War of Words: Men and Women Arguing*. On the rear cover it states that Mapstone set out to prove that women and men argue as equals, but ended up demonstrating the opposite.

Any suggestion that women and men have genetically different brains horrifies the modern conscience, for it seems to justify male prejudice. Our response to the accusation of prejudice is twofold. First, that we believe that difference does not imply inequality, and second, that any 'good or bad' genetic leadership dispositions we possess as individuals can be changed by good training and practice – if we are prepared to learn from others.

Our research study has taken us to the field of education, where it is now common knowledge that girls in the UK are outperforming boys in GCSE qualification grades to a level that we have never experienced before as a nation. There we found that the education system had adopted a teaching methodology that favoured the average female brain far more than the average male brain.

Modern teaching methods suit the girls more than the boys. Children in the modern classroom are rarely assessed in a competitive way – continuous assessment has triumphed over exam performance. Tests are set to measure overall school performance rather than that of the individual. There is little feedback on individual pupil performance. There are no league tables showing individual performance in each subject. Boys, however, need rapid feedback on how well or how badly they are doing.

There are other differences that make it harder for the boys to learn. Boys have short attention spans: they fidget. Almost every teacher will admit that boys are harder to teach than girls. At the age of 14, the average boy can only concentrate for 5 minutes at a time, compared to 15 minutes for the average girl – so boys need greater stimulus, variety and motivation to keep them working and to help them learn.

Over the past 20 years unstructured group learning has become the classroom norm – the girls, with their greater ability to concentrate and natural verbal skills, benefited from this approach. The boys have suffered. They find the emphasis on a verbal unstructured approach boring, which explains why so many of them are being turned off by the current education practices. Their brains are built for action and involvement, not for listening and talking.

A male friend of ours, a solicitor from a law firm in the City of London, was recently given the privilege, at company expense, of spending a week at Harvard listening to the best leadership speakers and management gurus in the world. The conference fee alone was $6,000. On his return to London he commented to us that *'I was shown no new leadership models that I could apply immediately at work. It was all talk about relationships. I didn't learn anything new on my trip to the States.'* This supports the contention that the male brain appears to need a structure and a form in order to learn.

We have presented the prizes to students from UK schools who take part in the Young Enterprise competition. The students, usually 16–18 years of age, form teams to create 'companies', invent a product and then market and finance its production. At county, regional and national finals the performance of the girls is far superior to the boys.

Girls outperform the boys in almost every aspect of the competition: from inner confidence, presentation skills, awareness of the effect they were having on others and relationships within teams. Mary Clements, one of the regional competition organisers from Cambridge, has remarked that *'the girls are so far out in front that it should be giving serious cause for concern in all sorts of places'*.

Many of the people we interviewed during our research asked not to be quoted. This subject has more than a hint of 'political incorrectness' about it. One example, taken from education, is the study that is under way today at both Oxford and Cambridge universities. In sharp contrast to the female domination of the academic results at GCSE level, both bodies are currently researching the reason why men are awarded disproportionately more first-class degrees than women.

This research builds on the work of Cambridge academic, Charles Goodhart, who was heavily criticised for pointing out that *'men get many more firsts – and thirds and failures. The women are bunched in the middle, they almost all get 2.1s or 2.2s.'* These are the facts, but the reasons that lie behind them are far harder to elucidate. Both universities currently stick rigidly to the final examination system, eschewing the modern trend for continuous assessment.

Although the results of the current investigations have yet to be published, we predict that there will be a chemical and genetic reason for the difference in the performances of the sexes. Male undergraduates with higher levels of testosterone, lower levels of serotonin and higher levels of dopamine in the brain may take more risks in their finals than their female counterparts. They may take more risks in deciding which subjects to revise and when answering questions in the final examinations. This may provide the answer to the conundrum of the greater spread of their results.

Our definition of leadership

There has been much debate and discussion throughout this century about how people become leaders. Leadership thinking tends to follow the evolution of organisations and communities. As organisations and communities evolved hierarchies, leadership developed a command and control methodology. Until the early 1960s leadership tuition was based on an examination of the actions of notable leaders from history. They were almost all men, and the belief was that leaders were born rather than made.

This view was challenged in the 1960s by a practical action-based approach that was effective in training people in the self-development of leadership skills and behaviours. This approach sat naturally and comfortably in heavily hierarchical organisations that had clear chains of command. Its epitome, and the one we have chosen to focus on, is Action-Centred Leadership, the famous three-circle model of task, team and individual. This was designed and built for the average male brain, a fact that is unsurprising, because it emanated from the Royal Military Academy at Sandhurst in 1964, which was then a totally male preserve.

This approach has given way in the 1990s to a transformational model of leadership, based on relationships and conversations. This purports to sit more comfortably in the flatter, team-based structures that are typical of the working environment today. Leadership training has swung, like the secondary education system, to a more feminine model. This has been based on distinction-based learning. Females, with their greater language skills and superior listening and visual skills, find it easier to articulate distinctions powerfully.

Complexity, chaos and connectedness were the scientific theories employed. 'Have a conversation' was the cry. Females are much better at having a conversation than males. 'Everything starts with a relationship' was the credo, and from relationships emerge more business opportunities. Females are better than males at establishing relationships. They read people better and have a better visual memory for detail. The average female brain is wired for this; the average male brain is not.

Our concern is that the leadership training methodology has swung too much towards feminine attributes. We are in danger of throwing out all that is good about masculine leadership attributes in the rush to embrace a more feminine leadership style. Admittedly, the majority of leaders at work in senior positions are currently male and therefore there is a logical reason behind the drive to get them to examine the way they think and behave as leaders. However, we believe that leadership tuition should embrace the best of both approaches.

The leadership challenge today is not to produce what is there already, nor is it to produce what would have happened anyway. The challenge is to recognise what is missing and then to invent a product, a service, or a combination of the two, to fill the identified gap. In today's competitive climate we need everyone to be a leader at whatever level he or she occupies in an organisation. From manager to receptionist, from van driver to chief executive, from accounts clerk to director, we need everyone to show initiative, irrespective of gender.

Our definition of leadership is a combination of a more feminine and relationship-based model: *'A reciprocal relationship between those who choose to lead and those who decide to follow'* (Kouzes & Posner) and the more masculine model that emphasises outcomes: *'Leadership is the achievement of results through others'* (Garnett).

Putting the two together, our definition becomes:

'Building a reciprocal relationship between those who choose to lead and those who decide to follow, in order to achieve an agreed common purpose.'

We have constructed an amalgam of the two approaches to produce a more complete leadership learning methodology that is based on the scientifically proven genetic strengths of both sexes:

Mainly masculine Traditional 'Old leadership'	Mainly feminine Modern 'New leadership'
1. Action	1. Connectivity
2. Task	2. Relationship
3. Fragmentation	3. Holistic
4. Competition	4. Partnership
5. Risk-taking	5. Paradox
6. Captain	6. Coach

◀ · ▶

Traditionally, the left-hand column would have been considered masculine or, more recently, 'old leadership'; and the right-hand column feminine or 'new leadership'. We advocate that the leader of the future will need to develop all of these distinctions, travelling between each pair of leadership traits as the situation demands. It is not a question of either one or the other; both are needed for complete leadership.

A complete leadership model

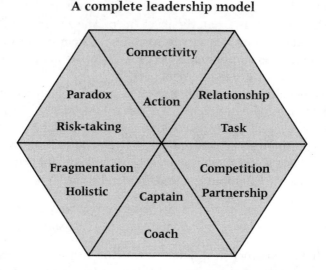

Women and men bring different perspectives, thinking, attributes and behaviours to the leadership situation, and each has much to learn from the opposite sex. The human sexes have different value sets. Men tend towards individuality, autonomy, rights, justice and agency. Women tend towards relational awareness, with an emphasis on communion, care and responsibility. We need the strengths of both sexes to counteract the weaknesses that each sex brings to the leadership equation.

References

Adair, J., *The Action Centred Leader*, The Industrial Society, 1988.

Carter, R., *Mapping the Mind*, Weidenfeld & Nicolson, 1998.

Channel 4 Television, three-part documentary *Why Men Don't Iron*, broadcast summer 1998.

Fielding, H., *Bridget Jones's Diary*, Picador, 1996.

Garnett, J., *The Work Challenge*, The Industrial Society, 1974.

Gee, M., *The Ice People*, Richard Cohen Books, 1998.

Kouzes, J. & Posner, B., *The Leadership Challenge*, Jossey-Bass Publishers, 1995.

Lawson, I., *Leaders for Tomorrow's Society*, The Industrial Society, 1999.

Mapstone, E., *War of Words: Men and Women Arguing*, Vintage, 1999.

Moir, A. & W., *Why Men Don't Iron*, Channel 4, HarperCollins, 1998.

Morris, D., *The Human Sexes*, Network Books, 1998.

Ridley, M., *The Red Queen*, Penguin, 1994.

Runge, Effective Leadership Programme, The Industrial Society.

3

Divided or united?

'We still think of a powerful man as a born leader and a powerful woman as an anomaly'

MARGARET ATWOOD

A question of perception

Physicists describe the world in which we live in one way, psychologists in quite another, while artists give us a different perspective altogether. Philosophers, through the centuries, have pondered the true meaning of existence and continue to do so today. Yet curiously enough we ordinary mortals have little difficulty in holding our own view of what we think of as reality. Our five senses of sight, hearing, smell, touch and taste give us a view of the world that we inhabit. Our world is solid enough for us to believe in. This solidity, however, has no base in science.

Physicists have proved the existence of a world beyond our five senses – a world of atoms, electrons and particles. We cannot see, touch, hear, smell or taste these phenomena using our normal senses. It takes a vast microscopic device for us to experience the mysterious sub-atomic world of particles.

However, even the best of science is made up of theories invented by mere mortals – human beings – and this makes all science fallible sooner or later. Science is no longer about the description of rigid and unchanging certainty. If, in the future, we inhabit other planets in the universe we will look back to the time when we were limited to just one planet, Earth, as a period of our primitive ancestry. Our perception of the solidity of the world we live in is both transitory and illusory when viewed over many centuries of time.

This view of solidity also depends upon our own unique perceptions. If two people go into the same garden, they may have two completely different perceptions of that garden. Brian's wife, Sue, sees their garden as a place to sit and enjoy the sunshine. She also enjoys gardening as a relaxing activity. Brian sees their garden as a place in which he contracts hay fever. The garden makes his eyes and nose run; to him it is an uncomfortable place.

Which of these perceptions is the right one? The correct answer is either both of them or neither of them, rather than one or the other. The garden exists differently for the hay-fever sufferer and the sun-worshipper. Both beauty and suffering are indeed in the eye of the beholder.

When many people see the world through the same set of values, it is as though everyone is looking through the same pair of spectacles. This is increasingly common today, given the widespread influence of the media. The collective paradigm that the media helps to create is very powerful and can often blind us to what is there. The problem with collective paradigms is that they tend to become inbred and rigid.

Perception and gender role

The way that human beings have looked at the relationships between the two sexes has not always been the way we look at this issue today. Depending upon one's individual perspective, the sexes today in the UK could be described as either 'different and unequal' or 'equal and the same'. When put on the spot, Brian would opt for the latter as being the view that prevails in the UK currently and Liz would choose the former. However, it has not always been like this.

Desmond Morris in *The Human Sexes* speculates that some tribes in West Africa still live as hunters and foragers in a similar way to our own ancestors. These tribes, he maintains, exercise a fair division of labour between the sexes. The males hunt animals and the females tend the children and gather plants for food.

He goes further by stating that this equality of food contribution is reflected in an equality in tribal decision-making. Men make decisions on male concerns. They decide on the types of weapon they wish to make and on the location of the campsite in relation to the hunting grounds they wish to visit. Women make decisions on female concerns. They decide on food-gathering locations, hut-building and camp layout.

The paramount need of our ancestors in prehistoric times was to survive, and survival was often precarious and difficult. The average life span of a human being was no more than 23 years. The human sexes depended upon each other for food, shelter, security and the survival of their genes through their offspring. Females spent a large proportion of their fertile years in pregnancy.

These basic needs motivated the human sexes to work together in partnership, because the satisfaction of these human requirements necessitated specialised gender skills and roles. Because this interdependent partnership between the sexes generated survival of the individual and the species, it automatically led to mutual appreciation and respect. Our ancestors never equated female and male; they balanced them. Morris concludes that the collective paradigm that prevailed during prehistoric times was that of *'different but equal'*.

Hunting and gathering, or foraging, economies lasted for more than 100,000 years before they gave way to horticultural economies, based on simple tools like the hoe. In these economies, men and women often worked side by side because it was possible for pregnant women to use the hoe. During these times it could also be said that the roles of the sexes were 'different but equal'.

Our own urban and industrial experience is a mere blink of an eye in the context of the evolution of our species. It is therefore only relatively recently in our history that one sex has become dominant over the other. Approximately 10,000 years ago horticultural economies gave way to agrarian societies based on the use of the plough. During these times it was not possible for a pregnant woman to handle and control an animal-drawn plough, or those who did risked miscarriage. So men went out to work the land and women stayed at home bringing up the children.

As agrarian production became more efficient this freed up some men, but not women (who were still engaged in childbirth and nurture), to undertake other roles in society. Men began to write, to draw, to build and to invent. The cumulative result was the industrial era, which was ushered in the western world in about 1760. This was followed by the urbanisation process as industry required labour in large clusters.

As these industrial and urbanisation processes engulfed western economies, the place of male employment was removed from the home. These developments in society continued to encourage reliance on the family as the primary and most cost-effective unit of labour production underpinning society. These factors contributed to what has been perceived by some as the relegation of the female to a secondary and subservient role.

Throughout history males have been absentee fathers and partners for a large proportion of time. But now men left the urban home every day to work in an industrialised centre rather than wandering in many different locations in pursuit of animals to hunt or land to plough. Because their workplace was fixed and men were gathered together, they took away the decision-making centre of society and made it their own. Women could not join men in this new industrialised workplace. They were left scattered and individually isolated in the urban home rearing children away from the societal centre where decisions were made.

A new collective paradigm of male dominance had emerged. This was based on the control of all the important economic, legal, governmental and societal decision-making. And this occurred simply because it was males who were present in the decision-making centre of the urban society. The females, who were concentrating on childcare and nurture, and thus ensuring the future of the species, were not. In contrast to the paradigm of *'different but equal'* that existed in our prehistoric past, a model of *'different and unequal'* emerged with the agrarian economies and was reinforced by the industrialised societies.

As more and more women entered the workplace in the second half of the twentieth century and the manufacturing base of the UK declined, equality of opportunity for women at work became a clamorous cry in society. This development plus advances in the efficiencies of contraception meant that women were no longer required to stay at home as nurturers and nest-makers. Equality legislation and political correctness in the last three decades of the century produced a new paradigm, which if not achieved yet at least should be an objective – namely *'equality and sameness'*.

The problem with the roles that the sexes play in society is that many people look at the map either through their own set of spectacles or through the collective paradigm that our society has created. Almost everyone we interviewed during our research for this book had a view about our work that emanated from their own perception that the sexes should be *'equal and the same'* or that they were *'different and unequal'*. Virtually no one accepted a position that the sexes could be *'different and equal'*.

Leadership and gender difference

We searched for two years to find these two statistically proven views that embrace both leadership and gender difference. There has been much material written on the subject and most books and articles have caused a plethora of opposing opinion. We were looking for surveys that indicated, without doubt, that there were differences in the ways in which women and men lead and follow others. Other surveys may exist; we do not presume our research to be all embracing.

Myers Briggs Type Indicator

The Myers Briggs Type Indicator (MBTI) is one of the most widely used psychological inventories in the world. Based on the work of C. G. Jung, the Swiss psychiatrist, into personality preferences, the MBTI has been taken by millions of people across the world. It has been translated into Japanese, French, German, Spanish and many other languages. The MBTI has been used for selection, promotion, teambuilding, self-knowledge and a host of other uses.

It highlights four pairs of personality preferences:

- Extraversion and Introversion – what is the source of our energy, outside ourselves or inside ourselves.
- Sensing and Intuition – how we gather information.
- Thinking and Feeling – how we make decisions.
- Judging and Perceiving – how we orient our lives.

The MBTI indicates to which of each of the pairs of personality preferences an individual is more aligned. The four indicators are then matched to produce one of 16 different personality types.

In only one of the pairs is there a gender bias. Across all of the millions of indicators taken, approximately two-thirds of males make their decisions by a thinking preference and a similar two-thirds of females make their decisions by a feeling preference. As decision-making is a fundamental part of leadership, this has immense implications for the difference in leadership styles adopted by men and women.

We have adapted the following from Kroeger and Thuesen, *Type Talk at Work*, from Lawrence, *People Types and Tiger Stripes* and from Myers and Myers, *Gifts Differing*. These illustrate decision-making process preferences, but we emphasise that they are only preferences. We stress that 'Thinking' types can and do feel and 'Feeling' types can and do think. Each personality type can be both emotional and intellectual.

Thinking types prefer to be logical, detached, analytical and driven by objective values in decision-making. These individuals tend not to get emotionally involved in a decision and would prefer that the consequences of the decision be their driving force whenever possible. People with thinking preferences are more likely to:

- be able to stay cool, calm and objective
- make impersonal judgements based on what is objectively truthful rather than on what is tactful

- enjoy arguing and proving a point for the sake of clarity
- be more firm-minded than gentle-hearted
- pride themselves on their objectivity despite the fact that others perceive them as unfriendly or antisocial
- divorce themselves from emotional concerns while making decisions and don't mind making difficult decisions
- think that it is more important to be right than to be liked
- be impressed with and lend credence to things that are logical, clear and precise.

The decision-making preferences of feeling types are driven by the interpersonal involvement that comes from a very different value set. The impact of the decision on other people is extremely important. Individuals with feeling preferences are likely to:

- consider a good decision to be one that takes the feelings of others into account
- naturally appreciate other people and their accomplishments.
- attend to relationships, putting themselves into the shoes of others to see their point of view
- choose tactfulness before truthfulness
- prefer harmony to clarity and logic
- be naturally friendly and co-operative, rather than competitive, in relationships
- think that it is more important to be liked than to be right.
- personalise issues and causes they care about rather than deal in abstract concepts.

The majority of women would seem to perceive the leadership task of decision-making in a different way to the majority of men. This is neither good nor bad, it is just a statement of difference. As Elizabeth Briggs, the author of the MBTI, has said, *'Everyone can develop a capability for the personality preference opposite to our own.'*

However, it is clear that for most of us in the UK the workplace is an environment where thinking preferences are much more highly valued than feeling preferences. The workplace for most leaders in industry and commerce is about margins, deadlines and punctuality. Traits such as objectivity and personal accountability support productivity, efficiency and profit. Indeed most of the female and male managers that have taken the MBTI are thinking preference types

Liberating leadership
The second survey we found was conducted by The Industrial Society and produced results that were totally unexpected by its designers. In 1996, the Society conducted research that involved interviewing and polling the opinions of followers rather than leaders. Followers were asked to identify and illustrate with examples the traits of the good leaders they had come across in any walk of life.

The result of this research was the launch of The Industrial Society's new 'Liberating Leadership' model in 1998. This model highlights 38 leadership behaviours and is reproduced in Appendix 1. They followed this up by introducing a leadership-profiling package by which UK leaders could undertake a 360-degree appraisal of their leadership strengths and weaknesses and then compare this to a national databank average.

We analysed the first 1,000 of these profiles and produced a gender split. The results are shown below.

Survey results

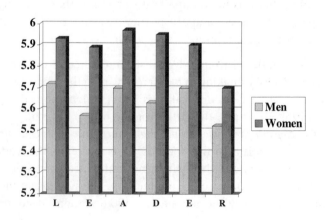

The Industrial Society groups the 38 identified leadership behaviours into six categories. The first grouping of six behaviours and attributes is nominated Liberates. Each of the six categories begins within the first letter of a word that together make up the word L.E.A.D.E.R. The others are Encourages, Achieves purpose, Develops people and teams, Example to others, Relationships built on trust.

At the time of our analysis, in late 1998, the survey consisted of 750 male and 250 female leaders from a large range of occupations. These included, *inter alia*, manufacturing, finance, the civil service, the voluntary sector, central and local government. The leaders surveyed are geographically dispersed widely throughout the UK. All levels from chief executive to junior management are included.

As you can see from the chart on the previous page, women leaders outperformed men significantly, scoring an average of 5% better than their male counterparts across all 38 factors. Staggeringly, women scored better in 37 of the 38 factors surveyed. Only in the single factor of being 'calm in a crisis' did men outscore women.

We recognise that there may be other factors involved in conducting a correct analysis of this result. Female leaders may claim that they have to be distinctly better than their male colleagues in order to be promoted. We conclude, however, that any survey which polls the opinions of others on a 360-degree basis must be relationship-based and, as such, will play to the strength of the relationship-building ability of the average female brain.

We are not so much concerned about the way things are as about the way people think they are. Women appear, on average, to make their decisions in a different way to men. They also appear, as leaders, to be able to create better relationships with colleagues at all levels in their own organisations than men.

Different and equal
In this chapter we have speculated over the variety of different paradigms regarding the role of the sexes that have existed

throughout time. In ancient times the paradigm could well have
been *'different but equal'*. Closer to our own time it could have been
described as *'different and unequal'*. In our own generation it might
be termed *'equal and the same'*.

We would like to suggest another paradigm regarding the
relationships between the sexes – that of 'different *and* equal'. Each
sex can bring different approaches, thinking patterns, attributes
and behaviours to the leadership process. Our contention is that
each should be valued for so doing. We should glory in the diversity
that each sex can bring to leadership and be prepared to learn from
one other.

References

Bronowski, J., *The Ascent of Man*, BBC, 1973.

Gray, J., *What Your Mother Couldn't Tell You and Your Father Didn't
    Know*, Vermillion, Ebury Press, 1994.

Kroeger, O. & Thuesen, J. M., *Type Talk at Work*, Tilden Press, 1992.

Lawrence, G., *People Types & Tiger Stripes*, Center of the Applications
    of Psychological Type Inc., Gainsville, Florida, 1996.

Magee, B., *The Story of Philosophy*, Dorling Kindersley, 1998.

Morris, D., *The Human Sexes*, Network Books, 1998.

Myers, I. B. & Myers, P. B., *Gifts Differing*, Davies-Black Publishing,
    Palo Alto, California, 1995.

Ozaniec, N., *Teach Yourself Meditation*, Hodder, 1997.

Turner, D., *Liberating Leadership*, The Industrial Society, 1998.

Wilbur, K., *A Brief History of Everything*, Newleaf, Gill & MacMillan,
    1996.

4

Are men and women different?

'If we are only open to those discoveries which will accord with what we already know, we might as well stay shut'

ALLAN WATTS

Putting things in boxes helps

It is fashionable today to state that we are all unique individuals. We, the authors, are proud to be different from each other and from any other human being on this planet. Our view, however, is that the human animal wants to see other human animals as representatives of groups. This we believe is a natural tendency since, as people, we must see the world as a series of patterns in order to make sense of it.

Our patterning ability enables us to recognise cycles, such as plankton yields conforming to a rigid four-year cycle of abundance and scarcity. We recognise sequences, like the order in which traffic lights change colour from red to red/amber to green and back through green, amber and red. We recognise processes, such as the 'right' way to mix the ingredients to make a cake.

We recognise shapes such as the stars in the sky that make up The Plough. We recognise similarities, like water going down the bath plughole in the same way across the whole of the northern hemisphere. We recognise probabilities, like the 14-million-to-1 shot of winning the UK national lottery. We recognise behaviours, such as the etiquette that demands no direct eye contact on a crowded London tube train.

As well as forming the basis of modern science, this patterning ability enables us all to deal with the daily onslaught of people and objects. It helps the living process if we can categorise. However, this natural and useful ability to see patterns of similarity also has unfortunate consequences. It can be offensive to reduce a man or a woman to a category, and it may also be misleading.

Gross quotes Edley and Wetherall in stating that debates in the nineteenth century about which sex was more intelligent were clearly more than just academic. Early attempts to prove that men's brains were larger and more powerful were just as much about justifying men's dominant position in society as about trying to discover the natural order of things.

The feminist movement has sought since the early 1970s to prove the dominance of the female form and brain. The male embryo form is indeed derived from the female, or more natural, form. However, feminists were out to use science to make a social and political point about the subordinate role of women in society, not just to advance the understanding of biology.

In 1986, The Industrial Society conducted a survey amongst male senior managers in the British insurance industry. It showed that 53% of male senior leaders thought women were inherently unsuitable for senior management positions in their industry. We recognise that some of today's male leaders reading this book could conclude that *'There you are, I've always known that women were not as logical as men and therefore they are only suitable for low-level jobs.'* We emphasise that this is not our intention. On the contrary, we maintain that women can be naturally superior at some essential aspects of leadership.

We accept that there are exceptions to every attempt at categorisation. However, patterns of similarity can and do help the exploration of progress.

Every culture makes a distinction between females and males

When meeting someone for the first time the first thing we notice about that individual is whether he or she is male or female. It is as though we need to have this information before we can interact with them appropriately. Most of us also expect other people to be able to identify us as a male or a female.

Our sex appears on nearly every official form. It is one of the facts that features prominently, and irrevocably, on our birth certificates. Although attempts are now being made to change this, our sex has, to date, been impossible to change on our birth certificates. We can change our given name by deed poll, but not the sex with which we were registered at birth.

The importance of sexual identity to our interactions with others is a reflection of the fact that every culture in the world makes a distinction between males and females. Our physical sex is recorded and validated on our passports and these documents enable us to travel abroad and to visit other cultures.

In the UK today advertising agencies, newspapers and magazines all recognise that there is a difference between the sexes, particularly in their purchasing patterns. They market some products to one sex rather than another. A lot of telephone services are aimed at women. A line from one particular television advert is *'90 minutes of chat costs only £1.35 with BT'*. Most men of our acquaintance would not know how to have 90 minutes of chat on the telephone. Until Brian met Liz, he had never had a 90-minute business conversation on the phone, let alone a 90-minute chat.

In contrast, the marketing of the Saab 9.5 is aimed exclusively at men: *'Keeping machines in the air taught us how to stick them on the ground. It is one of the most aerodynamically sophisticated cars ever designed. It is an impressive combination of physics and aesthetics. There should be no forces outside your control.'* These words are accompanied by pictures of aerodynamic formulae and combine to form a male image that is entirely foreign to Liz.

In spite of politically correct discussion and debate, *Women's Hour* still features daily on Radio 4. The *Daily Mail* rebuilt its circulation figures in the 1980s by appealing to female readers. Women's magazines have existed for decades, and in the 1990s have been joined on the bookstands by men's magazines like *Loaded*. Comics aimed at girl readers have always been different to those aimed at boys.

Biological differences?

Almost all human beings are built from a template that consists of 46 chromosomes. At conception, the 23 chromosomes in the egg from the mother are fused with another 23 that come from the father's sperm, to provide all of us with 23 pairs of chromosomes. One pair of these chromosomes is known as the sex chromosomes.

The female pair of sex hormones is XX and the male pair is XY. The mother's egg has a single X and the winning sperm couples the X of the egg with either an X or a Y. The Y chromosome is the key to masculinity, because it causes the production of high levels of androgens, male hormones, in the foetus. These male hormones switch on all the other 22 pairs of chromosomes that males and females share.

There are at least five separate biological categories in which men and women differ. They have different gonads and sex chromosomes; they possess different levels of the same hormones; they have different internal accessory organs and display different genitalia. Difference is a biological fact; equality is an ethical and social concept. The two statements are miles apart, separated both by faculty of academic study and by common human understanding.

Physical differences?

Physical gender difference can be measured in a number of ways. It begins at birth and lasts throughout life:

The male baby is, on average, longer and heavier than the female baby. The adult male body is larger than that of the female, being on average 10% heavier and 7% taller. Pathologists can identify the sex of long-dead corpses from the bone structure as well as the DNA.

In adulthood, the body of the male is, on average, 30% stronger than the female, with nearly twice the weight of muscular tissue. They have a higher ratio of muscle to fat than women. Males have an average of 26kg of muscle compared to 15kg for the average female. When the American armed forces started to admit women to combat units, in 1976, they found that women had only a third of the upper-body strength of the males and two-thirds of the leg strength. This is why the average female finds the physical exercise of the full body press-up more difficult than the average male.

Supporting this larger male muscle mass are a bigger heart and bigger lungs. There is more haemoglobin in the blood of the average male. The male has 20% more red corpuscles and therefore thicker and redder blood than the female. This means that men get more oxygen and have more energy. Men breathe more deeply than women, whereas women breathe more often than men.

The US marines have introduced 'gender-norming' for many of their physical-fitness tests. This means, for instance, that women can qualify by completing the three-mile run test in 31 minutes rather than the 28 minutes required of their male comrades, a difference of 9.3%. This is an indication of the greater lung capacity of the average male.

Females have a greater survivability quotient than males: they have a greater stamina to live. The biological vulnerability of the female, both before and after birth, is less than a male.

Although each pair of prospective parents may think that there is a 50:50 chance of a female or a male being conceived, in fact, there is a preponderance of males. Worldwide, approximately 120 males are conceived for every 100 females, but this ratio falls to 110:100 for foetuses that survive to the full term and is further reduced to 106:100 for live births.

More women survive to older ages: their average life expectancy is higher. In developed countries, the average life expectancy of a woman is seven years longer than that of a man. Even in the developing countries the difference is three years.

Males are more susceptible to heart disease, asphyxiation, palsy, convulsions, virus infections, ulcers, bronchitis, asthma and most forms of cancer. Men are 75% more likely to experience colour blindness, more likely to suffer from acute depression and more likely to commit suicide. There is no doubt that the female is medically the stronger and that the male is the more fragile sex.

It is the double XX chromosome that gives women the advantage. If the X chromosome from the mother has some genetic defect, there is every chance that the second X chromosome from the father will provide the cover and thus correct the defect. Men do not get this second chance.

Females have twice as much body fat as men – 25% of their body weight, compared to 12.5% for males. This gives them more resistance to famine and disease, in that they carry an extra emergency food store.

This fat is spread over the female's entire body in a thin layer under her skin providing an extra layer of insulation. This makes her warmer in winter and cooler in summer. It also makes it more difficult for her to lose weight than it is for him. Men also tend to have thicker skin than women and therefore they get wrinkles later in life than women.

Men's bones are arranged differently to women's. Men have broader shoulders and a narrower pelvis. The female pelvic girdle is wider than that of a male to allow her to give birth. The result is that males and females have different stride patterns. Broader shoulders and a narrower pelvis enable men to stride out with little wasted effort. The female walk involves more hip rotation, the wider pelvis forcing her to put more effort and movement into each stride that she takes.

Women have shorter vocal cords than men and the male larynx is a third larger than that of the female. The consequence being that men have deeper voices. Male vocal cords are 18mm long; female cords are only 13mm. The adult male voice averages 130–145 cycles per second; the female voice 230–255 cycles, one octave higher. The difference in pitch between the female and male laugh is even greater.

Males and females have differently shaped faces. Morris comments that the proof for this is to be found in the E-Fit identification system used today by modern police forces. Their computerised system has two sets of features, one male and the other female. Females have smaller noses, chins and jaws and thinner eyebrows than males. Males are equipped with more prominent jaws, bigger noses and more powerful brows.

Common sense tells us that nature has made the sexes different in physique. Most of us accept that physical sport, such as athletics, judo, rugby or football, should involve competition between adult males as a group and adult females as a separate group. This is a function of the different levels of height, muscular strength and lung capacity between the sexes. Many adult males and females would not want to compete physically with the opposite sex.

One theory, discussed in the early 1990s, maintained that as women's performances in sports such as athletics were improving more quickly than those of men, they would soon overtake men at events like the marathon. This has stubbornly refused to become a reality. The best male marathon performances are still a clear 10% better than those of the best females.

In contrast, it is interesting to ponder the fact that all of the early astronauts were men. Female astronauts had a weight advantage over men and always performed better at the tumbling and disorientation tests than their male companions. Logically, the first astronauts should have been women. They are the stronger sex medically: they weigh less and could cope better in the space domain.

Psychological differences?

There are three related but distinct ways in which psychologists view men and women. The first concerns the particular characteristics and behaviours thought to be masculine and feminine in specific cultures. These are called stereotypes. The second is self-perception, the degree to which the gender stereotypes are incorporated into men and women's concept of self. The third is gender-role ideology, the beliefs of the time concerning the proper roles and relationships that should exist between the two sexes.

Williams and Best state that although gender stereotypes represent only one of three ways in which the sexes differ psychologically, they are worthy of study. Gross bases a table in his book on the Williams and Best study. He lists the 100 stereotypes most commonly associated with males and females in over 30 countries. These range through aggressive, enterprising, inventive, reckless and tough for male-associated stereotypes; and through appreciative, forgiving, patient, talkative and warm for female-associated stereotypes.

In one of the largest reviews of the literature, Maccoby and Jacklin set out to show that many of the popular stereotypes about males and females are not borne out by the evidence. They concluded that there is a great deal of myth in both the popular and scientific views regarding some male/female differences. They discovered no consistent sex differences in traits such as achievement, motivation, sociability, suggestibility, self-esteem and cognitive style. They found the most convincing evidence related to aggressiveness, verbal and spatial ability, and mathematical reasoning.

In all cultures where aggression has been observed, they concluded that boys are more aggressive than girls, both physically and verbally. The differences manifest themselves as soon as social play begins. Male infants are more prone to bang and hammer objects and to make noise, whereas females are more subdued in their play. Young boys are more interested in running and jumping, fighting and both pulling and pushing. Girls tend to sit down and play with objects in front of them. Boys are more interested in investigating any new toy that is offered. Boy babies are more exploratory; girls are more cautious. Both sexes become less aggressive with age, but males remain the more aggressive sex throughout life.

It is well established that males are much more likely to be involved in delinquency, criminality and violence in general than females. The evidence comes from the analysis of any prison population in the world. In every prison, male inmates exceed females by a considerable margin. Even though female criminality is rising faster than its male equivalent, men continue to dominate the criminal population. Other findings, however, state the opposite. Durkin found that females sometimes score higher for certain kinds of indirect, non-physical aggression, and concluded that the aggression differences between the sexes were small.

According to Maccoby and Jacklin, girls' verbal abilities probably mature more rapidly in early life. From preschool to adolescence the sexes are very similar, but at the age of about 11 they begin to diverge and female superiority increases during the teens and maybe beyond. This superiority relates to both high-level verbal tasks, such as creative writing, and to low-level activities, such as spelling.

Further studies have shown that girls are better at verbal and communicatory tasks even as babies, while a number of other studies have shown no sex differences at all. Durkin, as with his findings about aggression, notes that the evidence is far from conclusive. He concludes that any difference in verbal ability is so small that it could be considered to be zero.

Do boys have greater spatial abilities than girls? Maccoby and Jacklin again say yes. They conclude that a difference does not exist in childhood but that it is present in adolescence and adulthood. However, they established that 25% of females score above the male mean score. Other studies have shown that boy babies have better spatial abilities than girls. Durkin again found the difference to be so small as to be meaningless.

Boys' mathematical abilities increase faster from the ages of 12 or 13, according to Maccoby and Jacklin. Hyde and Jenkins found that the differences were very small among the general population as opposed to students. Durkin suggests that the relatively late development of these small phenomena is a function of factors other than genetic ones.

After decades of research, the conclusions of the academic psychologists are therefore mixed. Some argue that the sexes are psychologically different and others that there are no proven differences between the sexes. The most recent thinking amongst the profession would favour a view that sex differences are exaggerated and that there is as much variation within each gender group as between the genders.

Popular psychology

In direct contrast to academic psychology, popular psychology books such as John Gray's *Men Are from Mars, Women Are from Venus* and Deborah Tannen's *You Just Don't Understand, Men and Women in Conversation* have become hits on the shelves in most bookshops and libraries.

Gray states that women like to talk through and share their feelings with others, whereas men go to their caves to solve problems alone. Men like to jump straight to solutions to both their own problems and those of others, whereas women like to share emotions before arriving at action-orientated solutions. Men want space in contrast to women, who want understanding.

Tannen contends that women speak and listen to a language of connectivity and intimacy, while men speak and listen to a language of status and independence. She contends that dialogue between the sexes can be likened to cross-cultural communication, prey to a clash of conversational styles.

She observes that men do not like asking for directions in a strange city. Even when they lose their bearings, flying an aeroplane, men are more reluctant than women to ask ground control for help and direction. Women get frustrated with their male partners who refuse to stop the car and ask passers-by to tell them the way. Males would prefer to drive around until their spatial abilities allow them to 'get their bearings'.

She goes further. Men are much less likely than women to ask questions in a public arena when the question is likely to reveal their own lack of knowledge. Men are more likely to start a negotiation process by stating *'This is what I want'*, women by saying *'What do you want?'* And this basic difference in approach and language makes the negotiation process fraught with misunderstandings.

Nurture as opposed to nature

Succinctly put, the nurturists' view states that a newborn baby is a blank sheet upon which parents and society can make an imprint. If the two sexes are treated the same as they grow up, then any perceived mental and behavioural differences will melt away. Kohlberg sums up this theory like this: '*I am a boy or a girl, I want to do boy or girl things. Therefore, the opportunity to do boy or girl things, and gain approval for so doing, is rewarded by parents, siblings and the society in which I live.*'

In this nurturist theory the child first comes to categorise himself or herself as a boy or as a girl, and only then will the child selectively identify with role models from the same sex. The child actively constructs its own sense of gender. Once it has acquired its own gender label, the child comes to value behaviours, objects and activities that are consistent with that label. Kohlberg believes that self-cognisance of gender takes place between the ages of two and three and a half years. He postulates that gender stability happens between three and a half and four and a half years and that gender constancy occurs from four and a half to seven years of age.

In direct contrast, Kuhn *et al.* concluded that two year-old boys prefer masculine toys like guns and vehicles before they have become aware that these are more appropriate for boys. Two year-old girls prefer feminine types of toys like dolls before they become aware of their femininity.

Finally, Maccoby concludes that by the age of three, boys prefer to avoid 'sissy' behaviours and girls to avoid 'tomboy' behaviours, and Money and Ehrhardt claim that gender reassignment is very difficult after the age of three.

Nurture and nature operating together

Our non-academic position is that nature and nurture work in the same direction. Nurture reinforces nature and enhances the biological differences that emerge from the average male and female brain.

Our view is that the average male child reaches naturally for the toy tractor, the average female child for the toy doll, and that this is the natural result of different brain chemistry. Many parents encourage this natural tendency, so making nature and nurture work in the same direction.

When parents seek to buck nature and try to influence child behaviour against the natural trend, they are often disappointed. Liz has a friend, Jane, who is determined to bring up her daughter without gender stereotyping and consequently, from birth, made sure that toys, TV programmes and education were not female biased. Today, Jane has not given up her attempt, but Amelia, aged six, now sleeps in a pink Barbie-doll bedroom of her own choosing.

Matt, another of Liz's friends, has a son, Jacob, aged six. He produced a Christmas list that contained only building, technology and sports toys:

Jacob's Christmas List

Rebound remote-control car
Telescope
Microscope
Electronic set
Turbo bubble bee yoyo
Metal detector

In direct contrast, here is the birthday present list of Brian's niece Alice, typed proudly on the domestic computer. She is also aged six; she has two older brothers and no sisters and therefore no sibling female role models. Her list shows all female type toys. Building, technology and sports toys are notable only by their absence:

Alice's Birthday List

Skipping rope
Cuddly dog
Black Ziggie
Emma Spice doll with dog
Rapunzel Barbie doll
Polly Pocket
A toy bike for Barbie
Fun song factory video
Locket to put a picture in
Doggy poster
Magic Dip painting

Love from Alice
XXXX

Further on in life, in education, we all choose the subjects that seem natural to us; girls, on average, choose different subjects to boys. At university, women are much more likely to study languages. Seventy percent of language students are female, compared to only 30% male, while 87% of students in engineering and technical courses are men, compared to only 13% women.

Furthermore, after leaving education, we all choose jobs that seem natural to us. And men and women, on the macro-economic scale, choose different jobs:

Male		Female	
Commercial airline pilot	99%	Dental nurse	100%
Nuclear engineers	98%	Nutritionist	94%
Architect	91%	Speech therapist	92%
Actuary	90%	Spanish teacher	78%
Physics teacher	82%	Social worker	72%

The left-hand column shows jobs that require some form of spatial ability. In the male brain the spatial function is located in the right frontal lobe. In contrast, the female brain uses both sides of the brain for this function, but as yet it has no measurable location. From tests and brain imagery, it is estimated that 85% of males and only 10% of females have good spatial ability.

The female brain has listening connections in both hemispheres, in contrast to the male brain, which has listening connections in the left hemisphere only. Her listening skills and verbal skills are better than those of the male. The right-hand column displays jobs that require a high degree of verbal and listening skills.

We maintain that each member of both sexes can be whatever he or she wants to be and can excel at whatever they choose. We also maintain that the sexes will choose to become different things and to excel at different tasks. We do not deny the importance of social constructs, but we also maintain that different brain engineering influences the career decisions we make.

In Sweden, which has been one of the more sexually egalitarian societies of the world for more than three decades, and the country which features at the top of Hofstede's femininity scale, the career choices of male and female children remain very different. Technical and mechanical jobs are still held predominantly by males, while social or people jobs are filled by females. Employment categories listed as building, construction, technology, workshop, woodwork and motor engineering still attract 94–98% male applicants. In contrast, employment categories labelled as social services, consumer studies, nursing and care attract 92–97% female applicants.

Sue Sharpe, in her comparative study of schoolgirls from the 1970s and the 1990s, found the same results in the UK. Girls were still not applying for the 'male' type of jobs, in spite of the equality encouragement they had been given in the last 20 years.

We recognise that employment patterns are changing as women increasingly take on more and more employment roles. However, some occupations remain stubbornly male. One hundred percent of stonemasons are still male, as are 100% of carpet fitters. Ninety percent of quantity surveyors are still male, and so are 97% of TV engineers. These are not jobs that have deliberately restricted female access; this is just evidence that some jobs are more suitable to the average male brain, that society encourages them to be done by males and men naturally choose to do them. Females, by and large, do not choose to earn their living these ways.

Furthermore, some jobs have become female domains. Eighty-eight percent of librarians are female, as are 69% of psychologists. These are not jobs that have deliberately restricted male access. Again, this is just evidence that some jobs are more suitable to the average female brain, that society encourages them to be done by females and females naturally choose to do them. Males, on average, do not choose this type of employment.

Brain differences?

The latest brain scans can reveal our thinking and our personal memories, both good and bad. Even our moods can be seen as clearly as an X-ray machine reveals the picture of our bones and muscles. Positron Emission Tomography and Magnetic Resonance Imaging allow scientists to locate the part of the brain that is activated when we perform a specific action or think a particular thought.

We can now see our brains operate 'live' on a screen. We can watch our own brain light up in one area when we register a joke and flash in another area when we recall an unhappy incident. We can see our fear being generated and measure the degree of pleasure we felt in response to a statement. We can see the listening connections begin to function as noises are fed through the ear. We can see how our brain tackles an object rotation problem.

From this imaging evidence it would appear that the brain of the average man and the average woman are indeed engineered differently. However, let us state clearly that not everything is different in the brains of the two sexes; in fact, as in the human body, most things in the human brain are identical. And let us be categorical that there are overlaps across and within each gender group.

As regards the human body, it is a true and fair generalisation to say that men are heavier than women. The average man is heavier than the average woman, but not all men are heavier than all women. The same spread applies to the functioning of the average male and the average female brain. It is a fact that the average woman has a wider and thicker bridge between the two halves of her brain than the average man. It is also true that there will be many women who have a narrower and thinner bridge than the man with the widest brain span.

Any suggestion that women and men have genetically different brains can seem to justify prejudice against women. After all, only a century ago the Victorians believed that men and women were so different that they did not even give women a say in society, and refused them the right to vote.

We have, unfortunately, lived in agrarian and urban societies where women have been subordinated to men. Women have had to fight and campaign to change this perception. The first 'suffragette' fight, which commenced before the First World War, was only concluded in 1928 when women attained parity in voting rights.

The second wave of feminist campaigners would claim that their objectives remain unfulfilled because women are still badly represented in the corridors of power, earn less and have less wealth, on average, than their male equivalents.

One reason why brain differences between the sexes is such a sensitive area is because of the fear of over-simplifying, and labelling one sex as being better in some way than the other. Ridley puts the point clearly and succinctly: if women are to allow men an agreed inch of scientifically proven difference, this will enable men to claim a mile of inequality bias – as they have done in the past.

We believe that these concerns are fair and understandable. However, we concur with Ridley, who concludes: *'Just because our ancestors exaggerated sex differences does not mean that they cannot exist. There is no* a priori *reason for assuming that the average woman and man have identical minds. No amount of wishing that it were not so, will make it so, if it is not so.'*

We stress that differences in the brain of the average man and the average woman are not indications from which to draw overall gender superiority in either direction. Most gender superiority claims are usually based on a false premise. For example, it is true and factual that 100% of professional Formula 1 drivers are currently male. However, it does not follow from this that all men make better and safer drivers than women. The statistics do not prove a male gender superiority claim.

A recent Reading University study commissioned by the Automobile Association shows that males are more likely to be killed in road accidents than women. They drive faster and break the law more often than women. Males have a higher proportion of accidents on bends, while overtaking and during the hours of darkness.

In contrast, women have a higher proportion of their accidents at junctions. Women, on average, have more minor accidents than men, but men have a greater number of more serious ones.

This survey concludes that the most striking feature of accident involvement across decades is the remarkable stability of the sex differences. Despite the fact that there has been a massive shift in the population of women drivers, there is little evidence that the sex difference in the pattern of accident involvement is changing over the years.

This does not make one sex better at driving than the other but it does show that they are different. The AA survey finishes with the statement that *'although the issue of sex differences is politically sensitive and scientifically complex... the explanation for these differences lies in the different behaviour and attitudes of men and women'*.

These differences in fatality risk and pattern of accident involvement line up with the differences in the brains of males and females. Men with a different chemical cocktail in the brain take more risks when driving than women, whereas women with fewer brain connections associated with spatial awareness than men have more accidents at junctions.

Male and female are not two mutually exclusive categories. There are many shades of grey between the brains of men and women and the attitudes and behaviours that result. There is nothing abnormal about a nurturing and caring male; just as there is nothing abnormal about a female aspiring to drive cars at incredible speed on a motor-racing circuit. However, the best individual male professional racing driver is always likely to be better than the best individual female racing driver. And this is related to different brain engineering as well as physical strength.

A hardware brain and a software mind

Science, by pointing out the differences in the brains of females and males, is opening a window on the reality of the human mind, a subject that has always intrigued the human race. Throughout history, scientists and medical practitioners have attempted to unravel the mysteries of the mind.

After one of our presentations on this subject we were approached by an individual who was irritated by our inclusion of the word 'mind' as opposed to the word 'brain'. He advised us to stick to 'brain' in future. This we have done, but only to avoid irritating a minority in our audiences.

The concept of the brain and mind as separate dates from René Descartes, the seventeenth-century French philosopher. He postulated that the mind existed in a separate sphere from the material universe, a concept that still lingers today. Although we can identify the part of the brain from which human functions such as laughter and pleasure emanate, we still cannot read the minds of others. Thoughts emanate from the mind and the only way that these thoughts can be communicated is through conversation.

The Descartes thesis was that only the material could be analysed by science and, because the mind was not material, it was of no interest to scientists. Their only interest should be in the brain.

This concept of the dualism of brain and mind was prevalent for centuries. But there were always scientists, like the American psychologist J. B. Watson who wrote *Behaviour* in 1914, who held that the mind and brain functions were one and the same.

This dualist view re-emerged in the 1940s when Karl Lashley, an American neurologist, persuaded most of his colleagues that higher cognitive functions, like conscience or imagination, were the result of 'mass action' by neurons and were therefore incapable of being precisely located in the brain.

We accept Carter's position that within the hardware of the brain is found the software of the mind. If the average brains of men and women are different, then we believe that it logically follows that they have different minds and will think and act in different ways when faced with the same problem, activity or set of circumstances.

The first known map of the human brain was produced on Egyptian papyrus and is thought to date from between 3000 and 2500 BC. The first recorded scientific tests that explored the differences in the brains of men and women were conducted in 1882 at the Museum of London by Francis Galton. Early research concentrated on brain-damaged individuals, and there were plenty of casualties of the First World War to provide a source of study. Soldiers with damaged left sides of the brain were shown to have more difficulty regaining speech and verbal functions. If the right side of the brain was damaged, they had more difficulty regaining spatial abilities.

This research continued with a study of stroke victims of both sexes, and gradually a picture emerged that enabled us to divide up the functions of the two halves of the brain. In 1962 Roger Sperry won a Nobel Prize for identifying that the two hemispheres of the brain were the homes to different intellectual functions.

The table overleaf, which is derived from Sperry's work, will be familiar to many of those who have been involved in leadership training during the last 20 years.

It was used to encourage leaders to use both sides of the brain when undertaking a creative leadership activity, such as creating a vision for an organisation, composing a speech or writing a report.

Today, brain scanning and its resultant imaging are beginning to show us just how precisely it is possible to identify and locate even the most sophisticated and complex machinations of the human brain. The location of specific activities in the brain shows how brain differences can now be linked to behaviour.

Left-hand side of the brain	Right-hand side of the brain
● Right side of the body.	● Left side of the body.
● Details.	● Creativity.
● Analysis.	● Visualisation.
● Systems and logic.	● Intuition.
● Short-term memory.	● Ideas.
● Facts.	● Imagination.
● Vocabulary and grammar.	● Long-term memory.
● Evaluation and criticism.	● Whole picture.
● Common sense.	● Body language.

We invite you to try the following brain test. It will indicate the degree to which you have a masculine or feminine brain. The test is taken from the book *Brainsex* by Ann Moir and David Jessel and has been mildly anglicised. It also appears in *Why Men Don't Listen & Women Can't Read Maps*. Parts of the test also feature in *The Brain Pack* by Ron Van der Meer and Ad Dudink.

The brain-wiring test[1]
This test is designed to indicate the femininity or masculinity of your brain patterns. There are no right or wrong answers. Please circle one statement for each question. This should reflect what is most likely to be true for you most of the time.

1.   When it comes to reading a map or an A–Z, do you:
a.   have difficulty and often ask for help
b.   turn it round to face the direction you are going
c.   have no difficulty reading maps or A–Z street directories.

2.   When you are cooking a complicated meal with the radio playing and a friend phones, do you:
a.   leave the radio on and continue cooking while talking on the phone

[1] Reproduced by permission of Penguin Books Ltd.

b. turn the radio off, talk and keep cooking

c. say you will call them back when you have finished cooking.

3. When friends are coming to visit and ask you for directions to your new house, do you:

a. draw a map with clear directions and send it to them or get someone else to explain how to get to you

b. ask them what landmarks they know and try to explain how to get to you

c. explain verbally how to get there: 'Take the M3 to the Basingstoke junction No. 6, go left at the roundabout and right at the second set of traffic lights'.

4. When explaining an idea or concept, are you more likely to:

a. use a pencil, paper and body language gestures

b. explain it verbally using body language and gestures

c. explain verbally, being clear and concise.

5. When coming home from the cinema after seeing great film, do you prefer to:

a. picture scenes from the film in your mind

b. talk about the scenes and what was said

c. quote mainly what was said in the film.

6. In a cinema, do you usually prefer to sit:

a. to the right side

b. anywhere, you don't mind where

c. to the left side of the cinema.

7. A friend has something mechanical that won't work. Do you:

a. sympathise and discuss how they feel about it

b. recommend someone reliable who can fix it

c. figure out how it works and attempt to fix it for them.

8. **You are in an unfamiliar place and someone asks you where North is. Do you:**

a. confess that you don't know

b. guess where it is after a bit of thought

c. point North without any difficulty.

9. **You've found a car-parking space but it is tight and you have to reverse into it. Would you:**

a. rather try and find another space

b. carefully attempt to back into it

c. reverse into it without any difficulty.

10. **You are watching TV when the telephone rings. Would you:**

a. answer the phone with the TV on

b. turn the TV down and then answer

c. turn the TV off, tell others to be quiet, and then answer.

11. **You've just heard a new song by your favourite artiste. Can you:**

a. sing some of the song afterwards without difficulty

b. sing some of it if it is a simple song

c. find it hard to recall how the song sounded but you might recall some of the words.

12. **You are best at predicting outcomes by:**

a. using intuition

b. making a decision based on both the available information and 'gut feel'

c. using facts, statistics and data.

13. **You've misplaced your keys. Would you:**

a. do something else until the answer occurs to you

b. do something else but keep trying to remember where you put them

c. mentally retrace your steps until you remember where you left them.

14. You are in a hotel room and you hear the sound of a distant siren. You:

a. can point straight to where it is coming from

b. could probably point to it if you concentrate

c. could not identify where it is coming from.

15. You go to a social meeting and are introduced to seven or eight new people. Next day you:

a. can easily picture their faces

b. would remember a few of their faces

c. would be more likely to remember names.

16. You want to go to the country for a holiday, but your partner wants to go the beach. To convince them that your idea is better, do you:

a. tell them how you feel: you love the countryside and the family has always had a good time there

b. tell them if they go to the countryside you'll be grateful and will be happy to go to the beach next time

c. use the facts: the country resort is closer, cheaper and better organised for leisure activities.

17. When planning your day's activities, do you usually:

a. write a list so that you can see what needs to be done

b. think of the things that you need to do

c. picture in your mind the people you will see, places that you will visit and things that you will be doing.

18. A friend has a personal problem and has come to discuss it with you. You:

a. are sympathetic and understanding

b. say that problems are never as bad as they seem and explain why

c. give suggestions and rational advice on how to solve the problem.

19. Two friends from different marriages are having a secret affair. How likely are you to spot it?
a.   you could spot it very easily
b.   you'd pick up clues half the time
c.   you would probably miss it.

20. What is life all about as you see it?
a.   having friends and living in harmony with those around you
b.   being friendly to others while maintaining personal independence
c.   achieving worthwhile goals, earning the respect of others and winning prestige and advancement.

21. Given the choice, you would prefer to work:
a.   in a team where people are compatible
b.   around others but maintaining your own space
c.   by yourself.

22. The books you prefer to read are:
a.   novels and fiction
b.   magazines and newspapers
c.   non-fiction, autobiographies.

23. When you go shopping, you tend to:
a.   often buy on impulse, particularly the special offers
b.   have a general plan but take it as it comes
c.   read the labels and compare costs.

24. You prefer to go to bed, wake up and eat meals:
a.   whenever you feel like it
b.   on a basic schedule but you are flexible
c.   at about the same time each day.

25. You've started a new job and met lots of new people on the staff. One of them phones you when you are at home. You would:

a.   find it easy to recognise their voice
b.   recognise it about half the time
c.   have difficulty identifying the voice.

26. What upsets you most when arguing with someone?
a.   their silence or lack of response
b.   when they won't see your point of view
c.   their probing or challenging questions and comments.

27. In school how did you feel about spelling tests and writing essays?
a.   you found them both fairly easy
b.   you were generally OK with one but not the other
c.   you weren't very good at either.

28. When it comes to dancing or aerobic exercise routines, you:
a.   can feel the music once you have learned the steps
b.   can do some exercises or dances, but get lost with others
c.   have difficulty keeping time or rhythm.

29. How good are you at identifying and mimicking animal sounds?
a.   not very good
b.   reasonable
c.   very good.

30. At the end of a long day, you usually prefer to:
a.   talk to friends or family about your day
b.   listen to others talk about their day
c.   read a paper, watch TV and not talk.

To score the test

Please add the number of A, B and C responses and use the following table to arrive at your final result:

For males
Number of As   x   10 points
Number of Bs   x   5 points
Number of Cs   x   (-5) points

Total points   _____

                                    _____

For females
Number of As   x   15 points
Number of Bs   x   5 points
Number of Cs   x   (-5) points

                                    _____

Total points

                                    _____

If you left any answers blank, please award yourself 5 points.
Please record your score on the graph opposite.

When we had our brains scanned Brian's brain was typically male and Liz's was averagely female. In the brain test, Liz scored 220 and Brian 30.

```
330
320    High – feminine brain
310
300 ─────────────────────────────────────
290
280
270
260
250
240
230
220
210
200
190
180 ─────────────────────────────────────
170
160    Area of overlap
150 ─────────────────────────────────────
140
130
120
110
100
 90
 80
 70
 60
 50
 40
 30
 20
 10
  0 ─────────────────────────────────────
−10    High – masculine brain
−20
−30
−40
```

References

AA Foundation for Road Safety Research, University of Reading, *Male and Female Drivers – How Different Are They?* AA, 1998.

Brothers, J. Dr, *What Every Woman Should Know About Men*, Granada, 1982.

Carter, R., *Mapping the Mind*, Weidenfeld & Nicolson, 1998.

Durkin, K., *Developmental Social Psychology*, Blackwell, 1995.

Edley, N. & Wetherall, M., *Men in Perspective: Practice, Power and Identity,* Prentice Hall/Harvester Wheatsheaf, 1995.

Gray, J., *Men Are from Mars, Women Are from Venus*, Thorsons, HarperCollins, 1992.

Gross, R., *Psychology: The Science of Mind and Behaviour*, Hodder & Stoughton, 1996.

Hofstede, G., *Culture's Consequences*, Sage Publications, 1980.

Hyde, T. S. & Jenkins, J. J., 'Recall for words: a function of semantic, graphic and syntactic orienting tasks', *Journal of Verbal Learning and Behaviour*, 1973, 12, 471–80.

Jones, S., *In the Blood: God, Genes and Destiny*, Flamingo, 1996.

Jost, A., 'Hormonal factors in the development of the male genital system', *The Human Testes*, New York, Plenum Press, 1970.

Kohlberg, L., 'A cognitive-developmental analysis of children's sex role concepts and attitudes', *The Development of Sex Differences*, E. E. Maccoby, Stanford University Press, 1966.

Kuhn, D., Nash, S C & Brooker, J A, 'Sex role concepts of two- and three-year olds', *Child Development*, 1978, 49, 445–51.

Maccoby, E. E., *The Development of Sex Differences*, 1967.

Maccoby, E. E. & Jacklin, C. N., *The Psychology of Sex Differences*, Stanford University Press, 1974.

Moir, A. & W., *Why Men Don't Iron*, Channel 4, HarperCollins, 1998.

Moir, A. & Jessel, D., *Brainsex*, Mandarin, 1996.

Money, J. & Ehrhardt, A. A., *Man and Woman, Boy and Girl*, Johns Hopkins University Press, 1972.

Morris, D., *The Human Sexes*, Network Books, 1998.

Pease, A. & B., *Why Men Don't Listen & Women Can't Read Maps*, PTI, 1999.

Ridley, M., *The Red Queen*, Penguin, 1994.

Sharpe, S., *Just Like a Girl*, Penguin, 1994.

Tannen, D., *You Just Don't Understand: Men & Women in Conversation*, Virago Press, 1992.

Van der Meer, R. & Dudink, A., *The Brain Pack*, Van der Meer Publishing, a division of PHPC, 1997.

Williams, J. E. & Best, D. L., 'Cross-cultural views of women and men', *Psychology & Culture*, ed. W. J. Lonner & R. S. Malplass, Boston, Alleyne & Bacon, 1994.

5

Leadership brainwaves

'He or she comes into the world with constructional, genetic and hormonally mediated ... behavioural biases and innate patterning'

M. DIAMOND

What follows in this chapter is our own lay interpretation of a complex subject that is still unfolding as we write. The science that has analysed brain differences is undeniable. What is more questionable is the translation of these differences into behavioural patterns. Our objective is not to exaggerate these differences, and it is certainly not to stereotype either sex. It is rather to examine the range of individual differences, apply them to the leadership process and then accommodate the differences in leadership training to give us all the optimum chance of success.

We stress the point that we are not denying the importance of social constructs in determining behaviour. It is our belief that we need to improve our understanding of why we are the way we are as human beings, which means taking an honest and objective look at ourselves, as men and as women, and making some sense of it. We need to probe into why we think and act the way we do. Above all, we believe that women and men need to ask 'why' of our lives.

There appear to be some mental tasks for which the majority of women are intrinsically better suited and some mental tasks that the majority of males are better equipped to perform. The reasons for these differences can now be seen using brain-imagery techniques. To ignore these images because of a 'politically correct' paradigm that it is sexist even to hint at gender differences is to do a disservice to both sexes.

We would like to remind you that when we refer to male and female in this chapter we are talking about a statistical tendency. Approximately 80–85% of males have masculinised brains and 90% of women have feminised brains. Within the structural, operational and chemical differences in the brain to which we refer, the range will be wider still. We are not trying to indicate that all men possess one type of brain and therefore act in a certain way, or that all women have one type of brain and therefore respond in a different way as a result.

The structural differences in the brain

The structural differences

Female	Male
• Slightly smaller in size.	• Slightly larger in size.
• More rods.	• More cones.
• Lose brain tissue later – lose memory and spatial ability.	• Lose brain tissue earlier – lose thinking and feeling ability.
• Thicker corpus callosum.	• Thinner corpus callosum.
• Smaller hypothalmic. nucleus.	• Larger hypothalmic nucleus.

The female brain is slightly smaller than that of the male but may be used rather more efficiently. Pease quotes work that has demonstrated that females have, on average, 4 billion fewer brain cells than males but that females record 3% higher in general intelligence tests.

Rods and cones are the light sensors in the brain. Greenfield identifies that the female has more rods in her brain, which means that she can see better in the dark especially at the red end of the spectrum. The male has more cones in his brain, which means that he can see better in daylight. More cones also give the male better distinction and appreciation of basic colours and better hand-eye co-ordination.

Nystrand states that men lose their brain tissue earlier in life than women, and overall they lose more of it. Men are particularly prone to tissue loss in the frontal and temporal lobes. These areas are concerned with thinking and feeling, and loss of tissue here is likely to cause irritability and other personality changes. Women tend to lose tissue in the hippocampus and parietal areas. These regions are more concerned with memory and visuo-spatial abilities, so women are more likely than men to have difficulty remembering things and finding their way about as they age.

The corpus callosum is the bridge between the right and left hemispheres of the brain. Ornstein was the first to identify that this band of tissue in females is larger, wider and placed further back in the structure than in males. Two other bridges which connect the unconscious areas of the brain, and another which connects the two halves of the thalamus, are also larger in the female brain.

The assumption is that the larger the corpus callosum and the other connecting bridges, the greater the number of fibres that connect the two hemispheres and, therefore, the more efficient the communication between them.

The hypothalmic nucleus is on average two-and-a-half times larger in the male brain than in the female brain. This nucleus contains more cells that are sensitive to androgens, male hormones, than any other part of the brain. This area receives signals from two nuclei, both of which are concerned with producing aggressive or assertive behaviour.

The operational differences in the brain

The operational differences	
Female	**Male**
• Both sides of the brain open when concentrating.	• Closes down one side of the brain when concentrating.
• Listening and visual connections on both sides.	• Listening and visual connections on left side only.
• Spatial connections on both sides but not in a measurable area.	• Spatial connections in the front right hemisphere only.

Females with a wider and thicker corpus callosum keep both sides of the brain open, even when concentrating. Brain-image studies show that men close down the left side of the brain when considering concepts and mathematical and spatial problems, using only an area in the front right hemisphere. In laboratory tests, using the right side of their brains only, males score higher than females at solving maze problems, judging perspectives, geometrical problems, architectural planning, spatial perception and rotating objects in their mind's eye.

The brain connections that enable us to judge distances and space are located in the right cerebral hemisphere. Brain scans show that this right hemisphere cortex is more developed in males, even as babies. The right side of the male brain develops more quickly in males than in females. Females have spatial connections in both hemispheres of the brain, but as yet science has not come up with a precise location for these connections.

This means that men have greater spatial awareness and hand-eye co-ordination than women, which makes them, on average, better engineers, advanced mathematicians and carpet-layers, better at ball games, reading maps upside down and parallel parking. Males also have a better sense of direction.

Females have to translate spatial concepts into verbal language to solve a problem of this type. For example, to parallel park, the average female brain has to translate the spatial problem into the verbal language of which way and how far to turn the steering wheel. We stress that this does not mean that women cannot learn to parallel park; rather, that they do not, on average, take to this activity as easily as men.

The female communicative brain area is larger and more active than its male equivalent. In the region of the cortex related to verbal fluency and short-term memory, the female brain has a 23% greater concentration of cells. She has listening connections on both sides of the brain and these areas show a 13% greater concentration of cells than a male.

She effortlessly transfers verbal information from one side of the brain to another through her wider and thicker corpus callosum. Males listen through neural connections in the left side of the brain only. As a result, women have superior verbal and listening skills and are better at languages.

The chemical differences in the brain

The chemical differences

Female	Male
• Higher serotonin.	• Lower serotonin.
• Lower dopamine.	• Higher dopamine.
• Low testosterone.	• Higher testosterone.
• No testosterone 'high/low'.	• Testosterone 'high/low'.
• Higher oxytocin.	• Lower oxytocin.

The average male and the average female have different levels of dopamine and serotonin in the brain. Men have higher levels of dopamine, which acts like an accelerator, or a wake-up call, in the brain. They have lower levels of serotonin, which acts like a set of brakes, or a warning bell, than females.

Men have higher levels of testosterone in the brain than women, which means that men are more competitive and aggressive; women put the feelings of others first. Men prefer the cut and thrust of debate; women favour discussion and dialogue.

Before competition, whether in sport, business or other life activities, men have higher anticipatory 'highs' than women. This is shown by the amount of testosterone in the brain, which can be measured by sampling saliva. After winning a competition men experience an 'afterglow' testosterone high, much higher than women. After losing a competition men have a much lower level of testosterone, a disappointment 'low', than women. Chemically, men need the rewards of winning and with this comes its corollary, the agony of defeat.

Oxytocin is made in the hypothalamus and is released as a result of stimulation to the skin or to the sexual and reproductive organs. It floods the brain during orgasm and in the final stages of childbirth, inducing feelings of attachment, nurturing, holding and touching that encourage pair bonding. It has been described as the 'relationship drug'.

Females have higher oxytocin levels than males. Oxytocin is the chemical pair-bonding agent between mother and child. In tests, blindfolded and ear-defended, women can identify their own child through using their other senses. Very few men can do this. Female infants have better hearing, touch and smell than males and these advantages last a lifetime. Females have a greater naturally occurring dose of the 'relationship drug'.

How might these brain differences influence the ways we choose to lead?

Relationship versus action orientation

Lower normal levels of testosterone, and lower levels before and after competition, plus higher levels of oxytocin mean that women define themselves more through relationships than men.

A man's brain is organised to do things. In extreme situations, under pressure or stress, Brian tends to want to do something to relieve tension. His mother could not believe that when he learned of the death of his grandfather, his first reaction was to mow her lawn. She wanted to talk about her feelings of loss, Brian needed to relieve his feelings of stress by doing something practical.

The male brain is built for action; the female brain is built for relationship-building through listening and talking. He does; she communicates. This shows up in the difference in levels of 'report' talk between the sexes. Tannen states that men tend to talk about, to 'report', what they have done or what they have achieved. To females this can sound like boasting.

In contrast she concludes that, for most women, conversation is primarily conducted through a language of 'rapport', which is about building relationships with others and establishing connections of understanding. Emphasis is placed on displaying similarities and matching experiences. Women show more empathy and flexibility in conversation than men.

We received this humorous Email from a colleague in New Zealand just before the final publishing deadline.

Scene set

Girl and boy have been having a relationship for about four months. One Friday night they meet in a bar after work. They stay for a few drinks, then go to get some food at a local restaurant near their respective apartments. They eat, then go back to his place and she stays over.

Her story

Well, Ed was in an odd mood when I got to the bar. I thought it might have been because I was a bit late, but he didn't say anything about it. The conversation was quite slow-going, so I suggested we go off somewhere more intimate so that we could talk more privately. So we went to this restaurant and he's still a bit funny, so I keep trying to cheer him up. I start to wonder whether it's me or something. So I ask him but he says no, but I'm not really sure. In the cab back to his house I say I love him and he just puts his arm around me, and I don't know what that means because he doesn't say anything back. When we get to his place I wonder if he is going off me, so I try to ask him but he just switches on the TV. So I say I'm going off to bed and after about ten minutes he joins me and we make love.

His story
Bad day at work. Great sex later.

Women like to talk, listen, discuss issues and get others involved. They come up with answers through sharing their thoughts and feelings. Sharing is important to women.

Research done by the UK's British Telecom illustrates that, on average, men spend only three to five minutes on personal telephone calls, whereas women spend twenty to twenty-five minutes in conversation. This would seem to support the view that women have more need to share than men and that they have the verbal skills to fulfil this biological need.

Focus and target orientation
The thinner corpus callosum of the male means that he shuts down half of his brain to concentrate, and this can be seen clearly on brain-imaging pictures. The male brain is compartmentalised. He uses only the hemisphere that is suited to the task in hand at the time: the right hemisphere for spatial problems and the left for language. Men's brains are organised to do one thing at a time. They find it difficult to do lots of different things at once. Males are more single-minded, focused and target-orientated than women.

Brian knows that he is focused and always has been. His wife also knows from long experience that, if she wants to talk meaningfully to him, she will only gain his full attention if the radio or television is switched off, or the book removed from his hand.

Multi-tasking

Imaging studies show that females keep both hemispheres of the brain open even when they are concentrating. When they undertake complex tasks there is a tendency for women to bring both sides of the brain into play at the same time. Females are better at multi-tasking and thinking about many different things at once.

Even when under the stress of lecturing, Liz finds herself thinking about other things. These thoughts can be as random as what to buy for tea or who she fancies in the audience. In contrast, Brian can only concentrate on the one task in hand. No stray thoughts occur to him while lecturing.

When cooking, Brian can create a risotto and a salad, but he does them sequentially. He does one, then the other. He finds it more difficult to do both tasks at the same time. Liz, however, has no such difficulty: she naturally performs both actions at the same time.

Competitiveness

Most people would accept that the male is the more aggressive sex. They are more prone to violence, criminality, murder, accidents and injury and more likely to play vigorous competitive sport than the female sex. This aggression, this competitiveness, comes from chemicals in the brain.

In business, sport and in life as a whole, it is men who are the competitors. Even in the gentle occupation of gardening, it is mostly men who enter competitions to grow the biggest onions. Male conversations and banter are very much about 'put-downs' and 'one-upmanship'. The House of Commons is a place of relentless barracking and bantering, of competitive debate with political rivals, and men still dominate this arena.

In 20 years of involvement in leadership training, Brian has always observed that if you give men a competitive task their engagement is far higher than if the trainer does not provide this stimulus. Further, if the trainer does not set up a competition, men are likely to invent rules to judge for themselves who has won and who has lost. This applies both to individual and team competitiveness. Men do co-operate but they co-operate to compete with other teams.

Inventiveness

Inventiveness is a male preserve. Ninety-nine percent of all patents for inventions are logged by men. Inventiveness means imagining changing things. It involves new ways of thinking about things, rather than people. It is firstly a totally right-brain activity in visualisation. Then it becomes a totally left-brain activity in logic, modelling and building. The different halves of the brain work alone and sequentially. Females, with both hemispheres of the brain open at the same time, find this harder to achieve than males.

The inventions that influence us most today are linked with information technology. Men perform better than women in laboratory tests at mathematical tasks involving abstract reasoning, especially conceptual geometry. Advanced computer science, which is built on a foundation of conceptual mathematics, is predominantly a male domain.

Social awareness

Higher levels of oxytocin and lower levels of testosterone mean that women are more open and more sociable. The Moirs conclude that women are warmer and friendlier. They are less argumentative and more co-operative. As a result, females excel at any job where people are important and where relationships need encouragement. They have better social integrative and interpersonal skills.

Autism is a psychiatric condition characterised by abnormally slow social and communicative development. It is usually associated with other forms of abnormality, such as physically rocking back and forth. Four times more males than females suffer from autism, and nine times more from Asperger's syndrome, which is 'pure' autism without other physical handicaps.

Women using both hemispheres of the brain at the same time are more aware of their own emotions and the emotions of others. The emotionally sensitive right hemisphere is able to pass more information to the analytical, linguistically talented left-hand hemisphere. This allows emotion to be more easily incorporated into speech and thought processes.

Interpersonal connections

Women are better at sensing the difference between what people say and what they mean. They are better at picking up the body language signals that display a person's true feelings. They smile more and gaze more directly at others. They interrupt less and are more likely to laugh at the jokes of others.

Men, using only half of their brain at any one time, are far less equipped to read the social and body language clues displayed by both sexes. Men find it harder to read the emotional temperature. In particular, they find it hard to read sadness in the faces of women. Men do not feel the empathy for the pain of others that women feel. Most men do not gravitate to being intensive care nurses. Their brains are just not wired for the job.

Appreciation of distinction

A female's visual skills can be likened to a floodlight. She has wider peripheral vision from side to side and up and down because she uses both sides of the brain for this function. She has visual and listening connections on both sides of the brain and a superior corpus callosum to transfer the images from the right hemisphere to the language left hemisphere.

She can picture the items in a room better than a male and will remember what people were wearing. This is why mothers often claim to have, or are accused by their families of having, 'eyes in the back of their heads!' Females notice the differences in the room, the body positions of the inhabitants and the difference in facial expressions when they turn around. Women are more prone to notice emotions and emotional changes.

Visioning ability

His visual skills are more like a spotlight, much more focused than hers. This is why he can never find his car keys or his socks when he needs them. And it explains why he opens the door of the refrigerator and shouts, 'Have we got any milk?'

He can focus on images in the distance, whether they be materially or conceptually distant. He has a telephoto lens, whereas she has a wide-angled lens. This focusing ability makes men better at envisioning the future than women.

Above all else, leadership is about constructing visions that give people hope for their organisation and for the part that they play within it. It is a vital leadership attribute and males have an edge in this arena. This is because a vision of the future is constructed by using the right side of the brain only. Males have the ability to close down the left hemisphere and focus on the future without interference from the present.

Logically proving the right answer

Using their left brain, men like structure and form. They prefer to break things down into their component parts, like an engineer or a physical scientist. They like things to be logical and they have a need to find the 'right answer'.

Car manufacturers employ staff to 'tear down' the vehicles of their competitors' new models. They completely disassemble the vehicles and then piece them back together again. From this they deduce cheaper ways of manufacture and better constructional techniques. Almost all staff in 'tear down shops' are male.

We have already referred to the sex differences in the results of the Myers Briggs Type Indicator. This shows that males have a much greater tendency to want to be right and to produce the right answer.

Appreciation of paradox

Women, using both sides of the brain at the same time, have less need to find the 'right answer' or to be 'right'. Because they use the feeling, right hemisphere at the same time as the analytical, left hemisphere, they can more easily accept an unstructured discussion that perhaps has no conclusion.

A paradox is defined as a statement that is seemingly absurd or contradictory but is really founded in truth. One example is that light is both a particle and a wave. Male scientists argued for centuries as to which was true before generally accepting that both could be true, at the same time.

To most women, if a solution does not feel right, even if it is logical, it is not right. They are more prepared to accept that there is more than one right answer to a particular problem. The female brain has a greater appreciation of paradox. They look for both what feels right and what is logically right – and often this can be two different things.

Dialogue and listening

Due to superior listening connections based in both hemispheres of the brain, women are better at remembering what people have said and they can listen to two conversations at the same time. They can listen to the television and talk simultaneously. In a restaurant they can pay attention to the conversation at their own table and listen to the conversations at other nearby tables.

A lower level of testosterone also means that they are much less likely to want to compete in conversation. Women brag or boast less. They are better listeners than men and listening forms one of the key ways in which we all learn as children and adults.

Many adult verbal difficulties, such as dysphasia, are predominantly masculine. Males are four times more likely to stammer than females. Dyslexia is mainly a male phenomenon. Mild dyslexia is five times more common in men, while severe dyslexia is ten times more common. Boys are also the main recipients of speech therapy.

Group working

Because the male only uses half of his brain at a time, the male brain boils over more easily when bombarded with detail and emotion. When this happens, he feels the need to be alone to work a problem through or to 'chill out', and ponder on it silently. She likes to consider problems in groups and talk them out.

Men may be good at public speaking but women are much better at discussing and dialogue. This may account for the fact that there are far more divorced women's groups than there are divorced men's groups, even though the potential population for each must logically be equal.

This, together with a lesser need to be right, makes women better at group work than men. Men are more focused on independence for themselves, women on intimacy with others. And both predilections are selfish, deriving from the genetic differences in the brain. However, the current societal paradigm makes the male behaviour appear more selfish than the female interest in intimacy.

Risk-taking

The chemical differences in the brain mean that men like taking more risks. They are more easily bored and more impatient, craving novelty and new experiences. They are more likely to be sensation seekers – driving fast cars and jumping out of planes. Once men have mastered a particular new experience they look for different ones. They search for the next promotion or the next job.

Men also cut more corners than women. Throughout life men are more likely to die of a violent accident than women. By the age of 30, in some countries, males are 15 times more likely to have died from an accident.

Men predominate in all of the high-risk professions. Men are the derivatives traders. Men predominate as members in all forms of serious gambling clubs.

The lower levels of dopamine and higher levels of serotonin in the average female brain mean that women like to consider all the options before making a decision. They will more naturally consult others to minimise the risk.

Coaching

The testosterone highs and lows that men experience before and after competition mean they will go for the 'kill' and for the 'deal' more aggressively than women. Men need heroes, and to become heroes, more than women.

Because women are less competitive and have more empathy than men, they can identify better with the objectives and goals of others. This, together with listening and visual connections on both sides of the brain, makes them much better at non-directive coaching than men. This may account for their increasing domination of the psychology and counselling professions in which the main focus is to get people to provide their own solutions to their own problems.

Status quo challenge

The wish to challenge the status quo derives from a high level of testosterone. Men endeavour to control the aggression and competitiveness created by their testosterone by inventing rules that provide for a more civilised society: for example, offside and foul in football, no ball and lbw in cricket, and the rules of warfare and the Geneva Convention in battle. Without these rules, the game, sport or battle would degenerate into pure barbarism and mayhem.

Most men define themselves through these rules as an essential of civilisation. Other men with more testosterone then try to break these rules. Rebellion against the status quo is a function of testosterone.

It is risky to challenge the accepted order of things, and men, thanks to lower levels of serotonin and higher levels of dopamine, are the greater risk-takers and therefore the greater challengers of the status quo.

Desire to become the best

Because of their testosterone, the rules of job and status mean much to men. This means that they create hierarchies, league tables and performance measurements to satisfy this biological need. In other words, they need to be able to judge themselves against the performance of other males. Men are biologically built to take part in team games in which one side wins and the other side loses. Men have the urge, as individuals and in teams, to be number one, to be the best.

They like political intrigue, challenge and conquest. Men play to win, and this natural trait automatically means that someone else loses. Men come naturally from the win/lose paradigm. Put two win/lose males together and a lose/lose situation can develop. Each is so concerned with not letting the other win that they would rather lose than let this happen. In contrast, women judge themselves much more against the concept of their own personal best rather than wanting to be simply the best.

Our different leadership gifts

We stress that we are not in the business of building gender stereotypes upon which to make leadership judgements. Our endeavour is to take the best from each sex to create the best possible leadership tuition package, and this should be to the benefit of leaders of both sexes.

Our interpretation is that the natural and genetic gifts that the average female and male brain brings to leadership are as follows:

Feminine	Masculine
1. Relationship orientation.	1. Action orientation.
2. Dialogue.	2. Competitiveness.
3. Listening.	3. Vision.
4. Coaching.	4. Inventiveness.
5. Appreciation of paradox.	5. Risk-taking.
6. Interpersonal connections.	6. Target orientation.
7. Social awareness.	7. Status quo challenge.
8. Group working.	8. Desire to be the best.
9. Multi-tasking.	9. Focus.
10. Appreciation of distinction.	10. Structure and form.

References

Brothers, J. Dr, *What Every Woman Should Know About Men*, Granada, 1982.

Carter, R., *Mapping the Mind*, Weidenfeld & Nicolson, 1998.

Coote, A. & Pattulo, P., *Power and Prejudice*, Weidenfeld & Nicolson, 1990.

Greenfield, S., *The Human Brain: A Guided Tour*, Phoenix, 1997.

Kroeger, O. & Thuesen, J. M., *Type Talk at Work,* Tilden Press, 1992.

Lawrence, G., *People Types & Tiger Stripes*, Center of the Applications of Psychological Type Inc., Gainsville, Florida, 1996.

LeVay, S., *The Sexual Brain*, MIT Press, 1994.

Moir, A. & W., *Why Men Don't Iron*, Channel 4, HarperCollins, 1998.

Morris, D., *The Human Sexes*, Network Books, 1998.

Nystrand, A., *New Discoveries on Sex Differences in the Brain*, National Institute for Ageing, Bethesda, 1996.

Ornstein, R., *The Psychology of Consciousness*, Penguin, 1975.

Pease, A. & B., *Why Men Don't Listen & Women Can't Read Maps*, PTI, 1999.

Tannen, D., *You Just Don't Understand, Men & Women in Conversation*, Virago Press, 1992.

Thomson, K., *Passion at Work*, Capstone, 1998.

Wilbur, K., *A Brief History of Everything*, Newleaf, Gill & MacMillan, 1996.

6

Partnership coaching

'If you deliberately plan to be less than you are capable of being, then I'll warn you that you will be unhappy for the rest of your life'

ABRAHAM MASLOW

Understanding why we are the way we are

We believe that leaders need to understand why people are the way they are. As a first step, leaders themselves should acquire this self-knowledge. Knowing oneself is vital. We can achieve self-knowledge by understanding what it takes for us to learn about ourselves. This involves being able to solicit and integrate feedback from others by continually keeping ourselves open to new experiences and information, and by having the ability to hear our own voice and see our own actions. If we can understand why we are the way we are, we can then improve on what we have already. We have thousands of unconnected neural connections in our brains. Our characters, which we tend to think of as fairly fixed and inviolate aspects of ourselves, are really a function of our brains. They are our brains and we can change our brains if we want to. We can learn to make new connections.

Stroke victims have shown that this is possible: speech and movement returns only when the brain has made new connections. A friend of Brian's has such poor eyesight that he cannot recognise an individual across a narrow country lane. In spite of having an average male brain, he has improved his listening skills to such a degree that he recognises people from the sound of their footsteps.

We can all develop new behaviours, skills and attitudes. Men can learn to iron and women can learn to parallel park. Men can learn to multi-task and women can learn more focus. To do so, we all need to learn what does not come naturally.

We believe that we need leaders who can think as others do; who can put themselves in the shoes of others; who can sit in their seat; who can see through their eyes. We need male leaders who can think and act in a feminine way, and female leaders who can think and act in a masculine way.

We must find a way forward that is:

- factually correct about the differences between the tendencies of males and females and
- puts these facts across in a non-threatening way.

The rest of this chapter outlines how we believe these two objectives can be achieved.

We emphasise again that the generic traits we have identified are generalisations and that there are overlaps across and within each gender group. It is a fact that the average woman has more listening connections in her brain than the average man and is, therefore, better at listening. It is also true that there will be many women who are worse at listening than a man who has assiduously practised his listening skills.

As we have seen, the average man has more testosterone in his brain than the average woman. This makes him more competitive in most situations than the average woman, but it does not imply that all men are more competitive than all women.

Partnership evaluation

There are four steps involved in using these generic gifts to their maximum effect in order to improve one's own leadership:

1. We have the permission and encouragement to be ourselves and play to our masculine or feminine strengths most of the time.

2. We need to be able to appreciate how the opposite sex thinks and acts. Our own way of looking at the world is not the only one available to us.
3. We must be able to use the gifts of the opposite sex when a situation requires them.
4. We need to identify our own shortcomings against the list of the 20 natural and genetic gifts and then develop them.

The real human being is in touch with minds other than their own. He needs to understand how her brain works and she needs to understand how his brain works. We all, as leaders, need to know which of the 20 connections are strongly wired into our brains and which we need to work on to develop. If we can achieve some development, however small, in all areas we can become better leaders.

To evaluate your own gifts, have a go at filling in the following questionnaire. Work with a colleague of the opposite sex who you know well and who knows you well. There are four stages and two parts to each stage. The two parts in each stage can happen concurrently:

First, take the masculine gifts, apply them to the male in the pair, and complete the relevant boxes. For example:

1. Brian completes the questionnaire, evaluating his own masculine gifts in column 1. 1 point is low and 10 points high.
2. At the same time, Liz completes column 2, evaluating her opinion of Brian's masculine gifts.

Second, take the masculine gifts and apply them to the female in the pair, and complete the relevant boxes:

3. Liz completes the questionnaire evaluating her own masculine gifts in column 3.
4. At the same time, Brian completes column 4, evaluating his opinion of Liz's masculine gifts.

Then compare the scores. Areas for development may come from the gifts that exhibit the biggest difference in the scores or from the areas where both individuals have recorded low scores.

Third, take the feminine gifts, apply them to the female in the pair, and complete the boxes:

5. Liz completes the questionnaire evaluating her own feminine gifts in column 1.
6. At the same time, Brian completes column 2, evaluating his opinion of Liz's feminine gifts.

Fourth, take the feminine gifts and apply them to the male in the pair, and complete the relevant boxes:

7. Brian completes the questionnaire, evaluating his own feminine gifts in column 3.
8. At the same time, Liz completes column 4, evaluating her opinion of Brian's feminine gifts.

Then compare the scores again. Areas for development may come from the gifts that exhibit the biggest difference in the scores or from the areas where both individuals have recorded low scores.

Partnership coaching – self-evaluation questionnaire

Questionnaire – Masculine	1–10 Male Column 1	1–10 Female Column 2	1–10 Female Column 3	1–10 Male Column 4
1. Action orientation				
2. Competitive				
3. Vision				
4. Inventiveness				
5. Risk-taking				
6. Target orientation				
7. Status quo challenge				
8. Desire to be the best				
9. Focus				
10. Structure and form				

Questionnaire – Feminine	1–10 Female Column 1	1–10 Male Column 2	1–10 Male Column 3	1–10 Female Column 4
1. Relationship orientation				
2. Dialogue				
3. Listening				
4. Coaching				
5. Appreciation of paradox				
6. Interpersonal connections				
7. Social awareness				
8. Group working				
9. Multi-tasking				
10. Appreciation of distinction				

Partnership coaching

We all need to show a willingness to learn what does not come naturally to us. The brain is like a muscle: if we exercise it, it remains in perfect working order. If we use the muscle to perfect new activities, skills and attitudes, it will become more adept at these activities.

We know that no one can become supremely good at all 20 leadership gifts – to think so would be idealistic. A right-handed person may never become as proficient at using their left hand as a left-handed person – but this does not mean that they should not practise using their left hand.

Brian knows that he will never become as proficient as Liz at relationship-building. She is supremely accomplished in this; it is, after all, the way she is naturally and is vital for the way she makes her living. This, however, does not stop Brian learning from her to become a more proficient leader himself.

To improve in our weak areas we need to understand what each of the leadership gifts means. We also need a process that allows us to practise each of the gifts. We have tried to construct each process so that it has four attributes:

- To encourage immediate action.
- To alter an existing practice.
- To ensure that it can be visualised.
- To be so clear in language that it can be understood on first seeing or hearing.

We also need a colleague of the opposite sex to coach us through our weaker areas. They bring newer insights into each of the leadership gifts than do colleagues of the same sex.

Getting started

There are a few things to consider before you rush off and find the first available, and willing, member of the opposite sex to partnership coach! Simply because you've found someone, it doesn't necessarily follow that they will make a natural coach. You need to identify someone who:

- has different 'gifts' from yours
- is self-aware
- you trust
- is an effective listener, and asks questions that make you think
- you could have a supportive relationship with
- learning would be fun with!

The role of the coach is to help another learn – it's about enhancing someone's ability to help themselves. It's about defining parameters within which to experiment. Above all, coaching focuses on future possibilities, not past mistakes.

Once you've decided on your coach you need to meet regularly in order to progress. A simple and effective framework to follow is the G.R.O.W. model:

Goal   – what is it that you specifically want to achieve?
                   – what are the measures?

Reality   – where are you now?
          – what are you capable of?
Options   – what are the possibilities?
          – how might the goal be achieved?
Will   – what will you do now?
          – action plan.

We suggest that you can use the practice and quick-fix ideas that follow to get you started. And we are sure that you will develop techniques of your own too.

Masculine leadership gifts

1. Action orientation

Definition
A predilection for doing things now or in the very short term. The satisfaction comes not from how you feel while doing; it comes afterwards, from how you feel having achieved.

Note
It is fundamentally an addiction to the testosterone 'high' of completing a task successfully.

Practice
- List your short- and longer-term goals.
- Choose a goal that means something to you.
- Analyse and model all the actions you think you need to take.
- Make a checklist of all of the necessary actions.
- Set and plan milestones that you know you can hit.
- Don't worry about how you feel, focus on the therapeutic result of the actions you are undertaking.
- Make sure that you hit the first ones you undertake.
- Take the first step, do something.
- Note by writing down your personal satisfaction of achieving completion and crossing it off your list of things to be done.

Quick-fix technique
- Examine the goals and lists of others who are good at this sort of thing and copy their approach.
- Promise yourself a special reward when you have completed the immediate task.

2. Competitive

Definition
Wanting to enter a race of your own choosing, knowing that others will be out to beat you, and relishing this challenge. It is about enjoying the competition for the sake of competition, because you know that this will bring out the best in you.

Note
It is an addiction to the anticipatory 'high' that comes before each competition and the 'afterglow' high that comes from winning. Whilst conceding that the 'agony of defeat' does exist, it does not allow this to affect the anticipation of winning.

Practice
- Enter one race of your choosing, be it in sport, business, the community, academia, the arts or socially.
- List the preparatory steps you need to take and make sure that you devote time to taking them.
- Prepare well for the race.
- Practise visualising yourself effortlessly participating to the very best of your ability.
- Constantly affirm to yourself 'I am good enough'.
- Focus on your own performance; don't worry about what others are feeling, doing or wearing. Don't focus on the performance of the competition.

Quick-fix technique
- Competition in most fields can be replaced in the short term by developing and having superb relationships with clients,

business colleagues, friends, etc. This may prevent you having to compete.

- Sooner or later, however, you will come across someone who wants to compete with you. You then have a choice, to accept the challenge and adopt the practices above, or to walk away. It is your responsibility to choose and to accept the consequences of your choice.

3. Vision

Definition

A vision is a dream that you have about fulfilling your potential – either for yourself, your team or your organisation. It is a set of words that is short, succinct, memorable and inspiring to you and the others involved. A vision is something that you can see. It does not contain a verb. Examples of visions put into words are:

- A land of milk and honey. (The twelve tribes of Israel)
- Absolutely Positively Overnight. (Federal Express)
- A one-woman show. (Victoria Wood)

Note

A vision comes from the right side of the brain only. Its creation involves closing down the left side of the brain.

Practice

- Think big – invent a future worth playing for.
- Although the vision must look impossible, it should not be an illusion, but rather a heartfelt desire.
- Imagine the future without the past.
- Visualise it without words, draw it.
- List all of the factors that are preventing you achieving your potential.
- Wipe the slate clean of all of these interferences by re-framing every negative thought into a positive statement.
- Throw away the lists of your interferences, keeping only the positive statements.

- Craft the words carefully and slowly over time and involve others, checking all the time to see what the picture you are creating means for them.
- When it is eventually agreed, write it up for all involved to see.
- Remind others of it and refer to it constantly.

Quick-fix technique
- Don't try to do this on your own if you are not good at this aspect. It is frustrating and it hurts.
- Work with someone else who is strongly connected to this predominantly masculine trait.

4. Inventiveness

Definition
This means coming up with something original. It is about more than making connections and then transferring ideas from one area of life and applying it to another. It involves both making connections and the conceptualisation of something that no one else has thought of before.

Note
It is an addiction to changing things, to novel experiences and new ways of thinking about things, not people. It is firstly a totally right-brain activity in visualisation. Then it becomes a totally left-brain activity in logic, modelling and building. The different halves of the brain work alone and sequentially.

Practice
- Distinguish powerfully how it is now: for example, by listing the characteristics of a pencil.
- Dispense with one distinction: for example, the characteristic of straightness.
- Substitute another 'off the wall' distinction: for example, that pencils are curved.
- Create practical benefits of that new distinction: for example,

curved pencils will not roll off desks and they will fit the hand better.

- Imagine new products or designs derived from the new benefits.
- Construct those products.

Quick-fix technique

- Look for connections in unusual places and apply them to your situation. Don't look for fashion ideas in a boutique; look at cubist art for ideas to camouflage tanks.

5. Risk-taking

Definition

Wanting to undertake a course of action where the future cannot be determined with certainty. At least one of the potential outcomes will be extremely beneficial to you; and at least one of the potential outcomes is frightening to you.

Note

A willingness to take risks is a function of low levels of serotonin and high levels of dopamine in the brain.

Practice

- Name three things that you would love to do but are afraid to try, whether they be at work, at home or in your leisure time.
- Say yes to one thing on the list that you would love to do.
- List all of the best and all of the worst outcomes.
- In weighing up the pros and cons, concentrate on the pros.
- List the actions necessary to achieve the chosen goal.
- Choose one of the actions.
- 'Seize the day' – go ahead, just do it.

Quick-fix technique

- Role-play with someone else in non-frightening situations to get you used to the thought processes involved.

6. Target orientation

Definition

Being able to fix a long-term target that you know you are able to hit and breaking that down into milestones that you know that you will meet along the way.

Note

This has the element of personal integrity attached. It means not only keeping promises to others but keeping promises to yourself.

Practice

- Set yourself targets that are SMART:
  - **S**pecific
  - **M**easurable
  - **A**ction orientated
  - **R**ealistic
  - **T**ime bound

- Make them real by writing them down and keeping them prominently on display: for example, on the wall in front of your desk, or in the front of your diary.
- Inform others that you have set yourself targets and ask them to assist you in monitoring them.

Quick-fix technique

- Write one target down in your diary and keep moving it forward until you have done it.
- Ask someone else to keep reminding you to carry out the act you promised.
- Then do the same with another target.

7. Status quo challenge

Definition

Being prepared to continuously improve a process, product or service. It can also apply to one's own habits, relationships and behaviours.

Note

This is again a function of high levels of testosterone in the brain. It involves challenging the rules and practices that may have existed for a long time. It can be an uncomfortable trait to adopt, involving elements of both mischievousness and persistence.

Practice

- Use the Japanese 5 'Why' technique. For every process, product and service ask why five times. You should then be down to the real reason the process exists.
- Establish the evidence for continuance of the current practice.
- If there is no evidence for continuance, establish a new status quo.
- Persuade others to go along with the new status quo.

Quick-fix technique

- Encourage others to disagree with current practices.

8. Desire to become the best

Definition

Passionately wanting to be and stay the best in the field in which you choose to excel. This involves competing with others and being prepared to measure yourself against the standards of others, which are constantly improving.

Note

This applies to individuals and to teams. It is impossible to be the best at everything you do, but you still want to try even though you know that this is illogical.

Practice

- Allow yourself to dream of potential accomplishments without negative distractions.
- Affirm 'I deserve to be the best'.

- Picture yourself holding the cup, the prize or the industry award.
- Anticipate the feeling of pride and achievement involved.
- Picture and anticipate what those close to you will feel about your success.
- List what you need to do, or to know, to be the best.
- Convert these into targets and milestones.
- Set out on the journey you have chosen.

Quick-fix technique
- Identify the best in your field and benchmark yourself against this 'best in class'.

9. Focus

Definition
Focus involves a searing 'laser-like' attention on one task or target. It applies to short-term targets and to long-term goals:

- Short term, it is about 'living in the moment', 'on the pitch', where the only thing that exists is the ball. Nothing else matters, all attention is on the ball.
- Longer term, it is defined as something that keeps you awake at night, something that is always at the back of your mind and that your subconscious keeps making connections with.

Note
This is a left-brain activity. It is about single-mindedness and can appear selfish. Chief executives commonly think about their organisation all of the time. Passionate and enthusiastic for their product, they are constantly thinking about how to improve things. They are continually 'turned on' to this thought process, and to make a conscious decision to 'turn off' and think about something else.

Practice
- Take the telephone off the hook or put the answerphone on.

- Focus on one thought or task for 5 minutes, then for 10 minutes, then for 15 minutes, and so on.
- As distracting thoughts come to you, mentally envisage them as pieces of paper and screw them up and place them in an imaginary waste-paper bin.
- Don't move until you have done or written something to your own satisfaction.

Quick-fix technique
- Remove all physical distractions and concentrate on doing one thing at a time for as long as it takes.

10. Structure and form

Definition
An inclination to put things into a logical order, knowing that this logic will have to stand the test of scrutiny by others who will be critically appraising the resultant document, model or concept.

Note
It reflects an addiction to explaining yourself and your thoughts to others. It is a left-brain activity only.

Practice
- Break the task down into bits and pieces.
- Put a number next to what comes first, second, and so on.
- Make sure that it has an introduction, a beginning, a middle, an end and a summary.
- Review and ask yourself, 'Is this logical?'
- Get someone else to review it critically before going public.

Quick-fix technique
- Get something down on paper and ask a colleague who is good at this to improve it.

Feminine leadership gifts

1. Relationship orientation

Definition

Relationship is the connection between two or more people. It is all about emotions and feelings, what is said and what is not said. The only tools we have to form, improve or repair a relationship are our speaking and listening.

To form a relationship, we need to bring it into existence – to invent it, to build it, to shape it. Very little is possible, in this world, without relationship.

Note

This can be a difficult concept for male brains to grasp. The focus has to be on the relationship for the sake of the relationship and only for the sake of the relationship. It is not a focus on what action or result you want to emerge from the relationship.

Practice

- Recognise that relationship takes time. This is not a quick-fix approach.
- It involves being there for people when they need you to be there, not when you need to be there.
- It involves always being true to your word. This is the concept of integrity. A trapeze artist makes an appointment with her colleague, in mid-air, at a very precise moment in time. If she fails to meet this appointment, no matter what the excuse, she has no integrity.
- Focus on what you are bringing to the relationship.
- Question whether the relationship is working and growing for both parties.

Quick-fix technique

- There is none. Relationships take time and effort to develop.

2. Dialogue

Definition

Dialogue involves a conversation between two or more people. It is more than just 'talking'. Dialogue exists when there is a purpose to the conversation.

Dialogue means wanting to see the whole amongst the parts of the situation and seeing the connections between the parts. It is about enquiring into personal assumptions and being willing to learn through disclosure. It means creating shared meaning amongst the participants.

Dialogue involves suspending judgement and releasing the need for specific outcomes. It requires authentic listening and a slower pace than usual, with an appreciation that silence is not threatening.

Note

This can be another difficult concept for the male brain to grasp. The focus has to be on the conversation, not on what people are going to do as a result of the conversation. It means being willing to challenge your own assumptions and not minding if others challenge them. You need to be willing to admit that you are wrong and that others know more than you do. Fundamentally, it involves removing competition from conversation.

Practice
- Be prepared to really listen, not just talk.
- Stand in the shoes of the other and ask, 'What is she really trying to say and how can I learn from it?'
- Identify possibilities in what is being said.
- Allow unexpected things to happen in conversation.
- Build on the conversations of others. Use techniques such as 'Yes, and ...' rather than 'Yes, but ...'.
- Play back the ideas of others in your own words to see whether you have understood what is being said.

Quick-fix technique

- Stop trying to be right.
- Smile when you recognise that you are trying to compete in a conversation and make others wrong.

3. Listening

Definition

Listening is much more than simply hearing. Most of us 'listen' from where we are – with our opinions – considering only how what the other person is saying will impact on us. We listen to agree or to disagree; to interrupt or to await our turn to speak; we listen for the flaw or for the recipe.

We need to listen to make connections, to understand where the other is coming from. We need to be able to stand where they stand and to see things through their eyes.

Note

The female brain has the advantage of being able to listen, really well, to two conversations at the same time. To males, because they can't do this naturally, this appears rude. It seems that she is not focusing on them alone.

Practice

- Look for areas of possibility for you.
- Judge content and not delivery.
- Hold your tongue, hold your fire.
- Listen for themes that show what the other is talking about.
- Take notes of what the other is saying.
- Display active body language.
- Resist distractions.
- Keep an agile mind.
- Keep an open mind.
- Listen between the words.

Quick-fix technique
- To help you practise focusing on one person, remove multi-conversation situations.

4. Coaching

Definition

Coaching means guiding another person to where they want to be! This is a selfless task. It means taking 'who the coach is' out of the equation. It is about helping others to win, rather than wanting to win personally.

Note

This can be directive or non-directive, depending on the style of the coach and the need of the individual being coached. Males usually try to coach directively: for example, by saying, 'This is where to put your feet and this is how you hold the golf club'. Some male, and most female, coaches achieve astonishing results using non-directive methods: for example, by saying, 'How did you feel on a scale of 10 about the drive you just made?'

Practice
- Allow time for others, be patient.
- Paint pictures for others of what they can be.
- Start from where the other person is, and review this detachedly.
- Support the trainee by being interested in him or her as a person.
- Listen authentically.
- Be aware and self-aware.
- Remove distractions.
- Encourage others to have a go.

Quick-fix technique
- Coach by numbers. Use a sheet of 'Tell me ...' questions that take you through the stages you need to go through. As you become more experienced, the flow of questions will come naturally.

5. Appreciation of paradox

Definition

An understanding that there is more than one right answer to every problem and in every situation. It involves the suspension of the very human (and somewhat masculine) need to be right.

Note

The female brain has the advantage of a thicker bridge between the left and right sides of the brain. This enables messages to flow effortlessly from the right-hand, feeling hemisphere to the analytical left hemisphere. If a solution does not feel right, even if it is logical, it is not right. Therefore, the female brain has a greater appreciation of paradox. They look for both what feels right and what is logically right – and often this can be two different things.

Practice

- Value the differences in people.
- Accept that yours is not the only view/idea/solution ... find a way forward from there.
- Practise using the right side of the brain: for example, by explaining how you feel.
- Use right-brain techniques like 'blue skying' and brainstorming.
- Keep Exocet missiles in their firing tubes.
- Allow competition between ideas, not people.

Quick-fix technique

- Ask other people what they think, and really listen to what they say.

6. Interpersonal connections

Definition

These concern the connections we make with others when we interact with people face to face. This includes our verbal and non-verbal messages.

Note

Women who use both sides of the brain in conversation find it easier to read the emotional temperature in both individuals and groups. They relate better than men.

We all make instant judgements about the people we meet. This is why the phrase *'You don't get a second chance to make a first impression'* gets wheeled out by every coach who is sending a trainee off to an interview. And often we are wrong in that first judgement.

Practice

- Ask a simple question: 'How do *you* feel?'
- Really listen to the answer without interruption.
- Show that you understand how they feel.
- Be prepared to disclose how you feel.
- Exercise intimacy in the conversation by being prepared to talk about emotion and needs.
- Make a connection with where the other person is emotionally.
- Think about your response and, in particular, the effect it will have on the other person – and adapt it to fit the situation.
- Show that you care.
- Make them feel special.
- Be prepared to give people a second chance to make a good impression on you.

Quick-fix technique

- Become more aware of the way you communicate with others.
- Shut up and listen!

7. Social awareness

Definition

Relating to people in all social situations, both in work and outside. This involves being conscious of what is happening all around: reading the signs that people give. It is all about being a good mixer.

Note

Women who use both sides of the brain in conversation find it easier to read the emotional temperature in both individuals and groups. Higher levels of oxytocin and serotonin and lower levels of testosterone in the brain mean that they relate with others better than men.

Practice

- Set the camera in your brain with a wide-angle lens.
- Notice what is going on around you.
- Recognise the gifts that everyone brings.
- Focus on people's faces and on what their body language is telling you.
- Be aware of the signals you get ... and act on them!

Quick-fix technique

- Smile!
- Remember people's names – it's important to them.

8. Group working

Definition

This is not teamworking. Teamworking is a group of people operating for and with a common purpose. Group working is a gathering of people without common purpose. A team has a team agenda; groups have individual agendas. People in groups tolerate each other; teams have a sense of urgency usually built through a sense of competition.

Note

The EU parliament is an example of a group rather than a team. There are individual agendas galore and the participants tolerate each other but do not always pull together – which is the essence of teamwork.

Women, with their focus on intimacy and predilection for people rather than things, find it more natural to work in groups.

Practice

- Encourage and support others in the group, even when you cannot see a reason for so doing.
- Focus on building relationships, rather than on action and results.
- Practise going with the flow of the conversation, even when you can't recognise a result or an outcome.
- Share with others, of yourself.

Quick-fix technique

- Listen and observe.
- Remember always to thank people both there and then and with a personally written note afterwards.

9. Multi-tasking

Definition

Doing several complicated things concurrently – and doing them well! It also involves getting into the natural flow of the various activities.

Note

This involves using both sides of the brain at the same time. It is sometimes difficult for the average male to achieve dexterity in this function.

Practice

- Watch and observe how others do this.
- Start doing several tasks that are important, but not urgent, at the same time.
- Switch from one to the other at ten-minute intervals.
- Recognise that this is difficult and expect progress to be slow.
- Reward yourself with something when you have achieved a small success.

Quick-fix technique

- Get in there and have a go. Get your brain to make new connections by forcing it to do several things – don't worry about doing them perfectly!

10. *Appreciation of distinction*

Definition

The ability to organise what you see and hear. A distinction is a way of organising what we see and hear, and it is created in language. The more distinctions we draw, the more power and access to possibility we have.

Note

Female brains tend to have visual and listening connections on both sides of the brain. They both see and hear more details than men. She has a wide-angle camera lens that extends both up and down and from side to side, plus a microphone that picks up sound over a long distance, in contrast to his more focused vision and hearing.

Practice

- There are things that I know and there are things that I know I don't know. There are also things that I don't know that I don't know. Acknowledge that there are things in the third category – *'I don't know, what I don't know'*.
- Turn these *'Don't knows'* into possibilities by creating them in sharp and succinct language.
- Use summaries and conclusions that start, *'What I mean by "x" is …'*.
- Once you know the distinction, be open to see, hear and feel the reactions to others about the distinction because they will be able to improve the distinction.

Quick-fix technique

- Open your eyes and ears to what is happening around you.
- Spot things that don't fit your normal patterns.

References

Bernstein, P. L., *Against the Gods*, John Wiley & Sons, 1998.

Brothers, J. Dr, *What Every Woman Should Know About Men*, Granada, 1982.

de Bono, E., *Opportunities*, Pelican, 1980.

Ellinor, L. & Gerard, G., *Dialogue*, John Wiley & Sons, 1998.

Greenfield, S., *The Human Brain: A Guided Tour*, Phoenix, 1997.

Moir, A. & W., *Why Men Don't Iron*, Channel 4, HarperCollins, 1998.

Ozaniec, N., *Teach Yourself Meditation*, Hodder, 1997.

Whitmore, J., *Coaching for Performance*, Nicholas Brealey, 1996.

7

Leadership – yesterday, today and tomorrow

'An invasion of armies can be resisted, but not an idea whose time has come'

VICTOR HUGO

Leadership has always been about an appreciation of the skills and attributes of others. Every individual will bring their own strengths and weaknesses to the way they choose to lead others. Our objective here is to demonstrate that, in our view, the leadership models of yesterday were based in a masculine paradigm, while the leadership models of today are associated more with femininity.

Let us be clear: this is by no means a complete analysis of all leadership models. We have considered theories, ideas and models that we see as the epitome of the message we have chosen to communicate. Our purpose is simply to illustrate where our thinking comes from and, more importantly, to show what caused us to think anew.

Looking to our past – at work in the 1970s

Our contention is that both the models and the leadership training methodology used in the 1970s were derived from, and intended for, albeit inadvertently, the average male brain.

This is not surprising because at work, men were the leaders. There were very few female bosses. Women were mainly followers who worked for pin money, certainly for less than their male counterparts. A common male belief, shared by some females, was that the woman's place was in the home looking after the family.

In 1952, Elizabeth Pepperell had started her work with The Industrial Society, a major independent training organisation, running completely separate development courses for women. By 1974, the common opening question to delegates was, *'Please list the factors impeding your progress as a person'*. Top of the list every time was the word *'Husband'*.

In the insurance company, where Brian worked at that time, discriminatory practices existed. Females were 'Local Staff' who filled low-level clerical roles. Males were 'Career Staff' who were employed from cradle to grave and were important enough to be transferred, at company expense, from one branch to another. This had the effect of depriving females of promotion opportunities.

With men in charge of all recruitment, he is ashamed to say that sexual harassment, as we know it today, was rife and women were employed as much for their looks as for their skills. The only (potential) common female advantage was that they retired at the age of 60, five years before the men, who retired at 65.

Masculine-orientated leadership

Leadership models and theories of the 1970s and early 80s were predominantly male orientated. The model of 'command and control' had stemmed from the armed forces during two world wars. The model was designed for and used in war, in the heat of battle. It was developed with the paradigm that, in such circumstances, soldiers could not be trusted in the heat of battle to do what was required of them.

Soldiers had to be commanded and controlled, and should not be allowed to think for themselves. This had some logic. If the soldier really took time out to think about what he was doing, there was a distinct chance that he would decide not to put his life on the line, and, in doing so, would cause the battle to be lost. This command and control leadership model was transferred to the workplace, where lives were not on the line.

In industry in the 1970s there was a need to recognise the vital role that leaders had to play at work, and believers in leadership as the future for the UK campaigned that the leader's job was to:

- help people achieve more than they thought they could
- get people to co-operate, instead of destroying industry and commerce by internal conflict
- lift people to their highest potential and free them of unnecessary and limiting restrictions.

The vehicle chosen for the campaign was called Action-Centred Leadership (ACL), which was developed and introduced by Dr John Adair, in 1964. It was designed in the all-male environment of the military academy at Sandhurst by a male for the training of other males.

Leadership was defined at that time as 'Achieving results through people'. This definition is typically masculine, in that it describes the output from leadership rather than the relationship between leaders and followers.

The leadership activities were defined as:

- defining and achieving the task
- building the team to do this
- developing, and satisfying the needs of, individuals within the team.

In leadership education at the time this approach sat alongside the popular Management by Objectives, the brainchild of Peter Drucker. Managers did things right and were efficient, while leaders did the right things and were effective. One managed things; and one led people. Leadership was perceived as more difficult than management because people answered back. Here is a justification for this action-orientated approach taken from *The Work Challenge*, written in 1974.

'For the last 50 years, industry and commerce have had the advantage of employing large numbers of men who had leadership experience and training in the Armed Forces. Those who were involved in either of the two World Wars got their experiences in the Services, while those who remained behind were

given leadership responsibilities at an earlier age than they would have received in peace time. Now [in 1974] *this ready-trained pool of leaders is no longer available. The need for industry and commerce, therefore, to do their own leadership training is more important than ever before.'*

It goes on:

'The training must concentrate on what the leader does, not what he needs to be. The objective is not to change an introvert into an extrovert. The leader can be just as effective as one or the other. What we need to do is to make certain that in his own way he carries out his leadership activities.'

Apart from the reference to only one sex – male – the accent of the above is solely on action. This approach concentrates on what the leader has to do. This is illustrative of typical male thought patterns. His brain is built for action, hers for listening and talking.

Here are Liz's comments following her own attendance at an ACL training session in the early 1980s:

'During the ACL course, I was given 10 minutes to sort some playing cards. Then another task to complete two jigsaws against the clock. Then, yet another, to build a tower with Lego bricks against profit incentives. In each of these exercises, my colleagues and I were in competition with another team and the results of the two teams were compared and contrasted. There was definitely a winner and a loser in each of these exercises.

'I analysed two male leadership performances portrayed in a war film. One leader failed and the second succeeded. One lost and the other won and became a hero. There was one sighting of a woman in the whole film. She was a nurse who wandered around in the background and didn't get to speak a line.

'In terms of feedback, the tutor, as a matter of policy, banned all comments about the personalities of the leader or the followers, or how individuals felt about what they had done or achieved. Feedback comments were about what I had done right and what I had done wrong in the leadership context. There seemed to be no areas of grey, it was all black and white.

'The programme ended with an action session. I was asked to commit to action, again in a very short time span, as a result of all the action-

orientated learning I had undertaken. I wanted to talk and discuss potential options, but I wasn't allowed to. I wanted to reflect and think things through, but again I wasn't allowed to. It was action and doing, action and doing all the way through.

'*As my brain is built for listening and talking, it is perhaps no wonder that I, as a woman, found Action-Centred Leadership to be a foreign language. This is an action-orientated male programme designed and built for the average male brain.*'

Throughout this period, leadership focused on structure and on tasks, on breaking things down into manageable pieces. The 1960s and 70s were the heyday of organisation and methods. Tasks were broken down into fragments and then analysed, often by time-and-motion experts.

There was a linear relationship between action and result. '*Inch by inch, it's a cinch – by the yard, it's hard*' was one of the training buzz phrases of the time. Contrast this to the need today, in the 1990s, for quantum leaps and paradigm shifts.

Telling and selling and top-down decision-making were the key influencing skills for the male leaders. The top-down decision-making model used was known as the '5 Cs'. The concept was broken down into five stages – a typically masculine predilection:

- Consider.
- Consult.
- Commit.
- Communicate.
- Check.

Many more structured pneumonics were used. One with sexist overtones was used to demonstrate the resources available to a leader.

This one was known as the '4 Ms':

- Money.
- Materials.
- Minutes.
- Manpower.

The only reference to relationships was a focus on 'walking the job'. Here are the six tips that were used as a guide to senior managers on how to 'walk the job':

- Invent a reason to be there.
- What you do there is more important than what you say.
- Ask about their job, don't talk about your job.
- Listen, don't just talk.
- Ask for suggestions on how things could be made better.
- Put any resultant actions through the line of management.

These are all actions written by males for males. The significant point is that male leaders had to be told how to show that they cared for the people who worked for them. Female leaders would not need a reason to go down to the office or shop floor and have a conversation – the idea of talking and listening comes more naturally to females.

Here is an amusing quotation about walking the job from that period:

> *'If managers feel that they can't go to the staff and talk about their problems because they would not be sincere, the answer is: ... Don't worry about feeling sincere, just go and talk to people about their problems because it is part of your job as a leader. You will become sincere soon enough when you learn what the problems are.'*

Most leadership training expressed the view that *'Through doing you become'*. Today, we would probably put this phrase the other way round. We would probably say that what we are communicates far more than what we say or do. The perceived beauty of this approach was that the sort of person you were mattered less than the actions you took as a leader.

This is not to criticise the action-orientated training approach of the 1970s to leadership. It was of its time and a tremendous success. It helped to re-establish the importance of leadership in the workplace. This period was also marked by the emergence of leadership as a skill that could be learned by anyone. This approach debunked the paradigm that leadership was an innate gift available only to those born with it – who, at that time, usually came from male public schools and Oxford and Cambridge universities.

Tens of thousands of managers benefited from the three-circle model in the two decades between 1966 and 1986. It was used successfully countless times in the classrooms of British industry and commerce. It even reached the syllabuses of business studies faculties in schools, colleges and universities. John Adair, the original designer of A C L, became the first professor of leadership to be appointed by a British university.

We stress that we do not wish to be critical of John Adair, or Sandhurst, in this exposé. The leadership training provided in the armed forces was, and is, first class. It goes far deeper than ACL. The leadership credo at Sandhurst is *'Serve to Lead'*. This indicates an understanding of leadership principles that go well beyond the practice and use that industry and commerce made of ACL in the 1970s.

ACL was a quick-fix solution to an industry need at that time. It did not pretend to go into the depth of leadership training in the services. The quick-fix mentality is a predominantly masculine behaviour trait. It could be epitomised by the Nike advertising slogan *'Just do it'*. Males, in general, tend to prefer a simple solution.

We stress that our only criticism of ACL is that it does not sit easily with the average female brain. Female leaders, in general, found it hard to relate to.

So, we would summarise the masculine leadership paradigm of the time as:

The masculine leadership paradigm

- Services derived.
- Action orientated.
- Left-brain thinking.
- Engineering based with a bias towards logic.
- Linearity.
- Cause and effect.
- Unemotional.
- Leading from the front.

In a nutshell, the leader of yesterday was a male, left-brained, action-orientated soldier/engineer, who acted logically and unemotionally and led from the front. Here is our representation of the masculine leadership paradigm emanating from the 1970s:

Masculine leadership paradigm

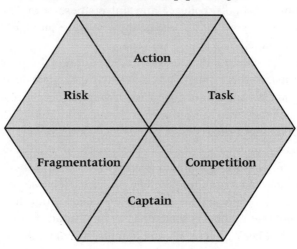

Many males assumed, and some still assume, that this action-based model is the only way to lead others. Some females have assumed, and still assume, that the only way to lead is to adopt male characteristics and leadership models. In other words, to compete in a male-dominated world of work.

We draw a parallel between this action-based approach and physics. Sir Isaac Newton had defined the laws of gravity and force into a theory that was adequate for his time. However, the enormous power locked within the atom remained untapped until Albert Einstein found the key. In his autobiographical notes, Einstein writes:

'Newton, forgive me. You found the only way that, in your day, was at all possible for a man of the highest powers of intellect and creativity. The concepts that you created still dominate the way we think in physics, although we now know that they must be replaced by others further

removed from the sphere of immediate experience if we want to try for a
more profound understanding of the way things are related.'

If you want to understand physics, you must understand
Newton's law of gravity. In the same way, we recommend that if
you want to understand leadership, as a man or as a woman, you
must understand the masculine-oriented paradigm. Women
leaders, in particular, need to know how the male brain works, and
there is probably no better illustration of the male brain at work
than ACL.

As time moved on inexorably through the 1980s into the 1990s,
other leadership models and behaviours began to come to the fore.
The expectations of leadership behaviour were shifting towards
those qualities traditionally associated with femininity. The lights
were beginning to go down on the popularity of the masculine
leadership paradigm.

The way it is today at work

The 1990s gave us a new social and political climate. Other factors,
as well as gender-role realignment, were having an impact in the
workplace. Part-time working was on the increase, rising by 25%
between 1978 and 1994. A self-employed sector had emerged
representing 11% of the economically active workforce.

The workplace was becoming more feminised. More women
went out to work and stayed in the workplace for longer. They
were marrying and having children later in life. The divorce rate
was also increasing dramatically, which meant that women had
to become economically independent.

As the age of industrialisation was coming to an end in the UK,
to be replaced by the age of information, a prevalence of office
work, social work and an expanding retail sector emerged. The
impact of information technology was being felt. This, together
with the demise of the manufacturing base, meant that different
skills were required – and females had the dexterity and the caring
skills for these new jobs. They were also more flexible, being more
prepared to work on a part-time or self-employed basis than many

men. It is predicted that, for the first time, females in employment will outnumber men, representing 56% of those who are economically active in the UK by 2004.

With more women at work their economic power and independence was growing, giving them a more powerful say as consumers. Television and newspapers, in the light of falling circulation, were actively selling to female readers and viewers. The education system had adopted a new education methodology – greater communication skills were needed and the girls at school had started to outperform the boys. The new 'laddettism' epitomised by the Spice Girls had begun to emerge. The lyrics in the songs they sang stated explicitly that the old subordinate role of women was over.

The numbers of women graduating from universities in the 1980s had increased dramatically. Female applications for university places exceeded those from males for the first time in 1991. Upon entering the workplace, women wanted leadership roles and, if they did not get them, they at least wanted a say in who got the responsible and well-paid jobs.

Other factors too were influencing UK society. The pace of change was accelerating. The term globalisation came to the fore. There was no more 'Little England'; the UK was part of the much wider society of the European Union, and the influence of the American predilection for consumerism and litigation was altering our lives.

Also born in the USA, the terms complexity and connectedness were being heard and used for the first time in the UK. There was a realisation that today's problems couldn't be solved with yesterday's thinking – the world was moving too quickly. Newtonian, or linear, thinking had worked well when the world was less complex. New types of thinking were required – thinking that would keep us ahead of the game and allow for creation. The challenge facing leaders in the 1990s was how to think differently about the business world they lived in. As scientists made breakthroughs that were responsible for generating massive technological changes that reshaped the life of everyone, business leaders struggled to integrate this new thinking into leadership models.

For many women, leadership training and literature in the 1970s and 1980s had been all about how to adapt, to cope, to power dress, to be assertive and generally fit into a masculine work culture. The result was too many Margaret Thatcher clones – a woman who epitomised the adoption of a masculine leadership paradigm by a female leader.

Is the future female?

As many women became determined to succeed as leaders at work, they recognised that the old male leadership practices did not naturally suit them. So, rather than trying to act as 'Superwoman' and continuously attempt to be something that they were not, they allowed themselves to be different. They no longer wanted to behave like men at work.

As more women were achieving leadership roles, they started to realise the importance of replacing the male-orientated models of the past. As a woman at work, Liz often wanted to say to the guys, *'Look, I have great leadership skills too, but I just can't be the way you are, I can't do it the way you do it. I'm going to do it my way!'*

In the leadership and management debate, Stephen Covey, with *The Seven Habits of Highly Effective People*, and Peter Senge, with *The Fifth Discipline*, had written their first books. These generated a plethora of others. This newer way of thinking about the leadership process was beginning to make an impact on enlightened managers.

We started to recognise that emotions played an important role in your success as a leader. Daniel Goleman had written his book *Emotional Intelligence*, and qualities such as self-awareness, persistence, empathy and social deftness were identified as important behaviours in leading organisations. Organisations were beginning to recognise that the human condition at work was important. Many people had led a Jekyll and Hyde existence – being one person for family and friends and another person in their place of work.

There were new insights into the architecture of the brain. Tony Buzan had popularised the notion of the left and right brain and applied this to the leadership process. The notion of managing from the left and leading from the right was beginning to emerge. This suited female thinking, as they have both hemispheres of the brain open most of the time. They are also better at recognising this as a paradox and at being able to do several things at the same time.

As these new philosophies, attitudes and skills emerged as vital to organisations, some women began to flourish because these are all qualities, ways of thinking and being, which women have in abundance. The hard shell of a male-dominated work environment was being chipped away. With one or two exceptions, like Margaret Wheatley, it was male authors, management gurus and lecturers who recognised *'that the old ways of doing things around here'* weren't going to serve them well in the future world of work. It was men who started to declare that the future was female!

The implication was that the old male way of doing things was wrong, and, if you want to survive, if you want your company or the economy or the planet to survive, you're going to have to think and behave more like a female. Much of the debate in the 1990s spent time persuading leaders that it was good to be female – and that it was men who needed to change their leadership style. What Liz found frustrating was that it was men who started telling her how she should behave more like a female; teaching her the value of thinking like a female!

The justifications the 'enlightened male gurus' used for adopting this natural female behaviour are drawn from anywhere but the true source. They quote examples from quantum and metaphysics, from new biology, from the eastern religions, and from nature. And the justifications all come from sources which the male brain will naturally regard as true – all left-brain logic and science. The true source of all these theories – the female brain – is never acknowledged.

The leadership paradigm was being feminised and models and ideas based on the importance of relationship were starting to emerge.

Feminine-orientated leadership

So, leadership of the 1990s was moving towards being female orientated. Training and learning methodology took on a whole new emphasis – involving a high degree of sharing of feelings.

Leadership models of the 1990s put the emphasis on good leadership at a relationship level. From the world of chaos theory and complex adaptive systems the ideas of dialogue, enquiry and the nature of human existence came to the fore in leadership thinking. It was about 'being' a leader. Leadership was seen to derive from a sense of inner values more than a tool kit of learned skills.

We conclude that leadership thinking of this time was based around eight key factors.

1. Distinction-based learning

A distinction is a way of organising what we see. It is created in language and allows us to see an increased range of what is possible. The more distinctions we have available, the greater the number of possibilities we can create. Females, with their greater language, listening and visual skills, find it easier to articulate distinctions more powerfully than males.

2. Relationship-building

Everything in the universe starts with a relationship. Most human beings cannot exist alone. We need other people to share our lives. We need relationships, and these relationships demand conversations. Under the tutelage of the old masculine leadership models, employees would have been criticised for having conversations at work with colleagues and indeed with customers – this would have been seen as gossip and to serve no purpose. The newer leadership models of the 1990s encouraged conversations and time spent on talking and listening to other people.

Conversations, however, are not limited to the exchange of words. Giving flowers is a conversation. Paying attention is a conversation. Real conversations mean standing boldly for what you believe and openly listening to others who matter to you.

If we want to call forth action from others, the essence of leadership, we have to have a meaningful conversation. If the action involves change, then the conversation must become even more meaningful.

3. Less control, more openness

Leaders were being encouraged to develop the space for others to show up in: to act as the coach, who was not on the field of play but who advised, counselled and encouraged others to succeed and fulfil their potential. Leaders were being encouraged to lead from behind. Team learning was encouraged, which involved an interaction between team members in the learning process. It meant talking problems through.

Women, who are more used to conversational dialogue, talking through their problems and gravitating towards intimacy rather than independence, found these newer leadership practices easier to adopt.

4. Authentic listening

Authentic listening requires that you listen for the opportunity in what is being said. It means asking the question, *'What do they see that I don't?'* As leaders, we underestimate the value of the quality of our listening. This affects our ability to access information from others. As Covey has put it so well, *'Seek first to understand and only then seek to be understood.'*

A female's communicative brain area is larger. Listening connections are more in tune and cells operating from both sides of the brain are larger and more active. Therefore, females find it easier to listen – not simply to the words but also to read the body language and non-verbal signs. This makes it easier for them to show empathy. They are naturally better at authentic listening.

5. Values driven

Instead of growth, results and time being the measures of achievement, ethics, principles and values were emerging as drivers and motivators for organisations. With the realisation that we needed the whole human being to come to work, organisations had to balance those personal and organisational values.

6. 'Being' a leader

Up until now, the emphasis had been on what you do as a leader. Doing more equalled getting more. The new sciences and writers instead put the emphasis on how you 'be' a leader – the importance of your own self-actualisation. This was taken from ontology, the branch of metaphysics which dealt with the very nature and essence of things and their relationship to the universe.

Females, with their greater listening and conversational skills and their predilection for discussing things in groups, are more open to sharing and exploring who they are: they are happier than men at exploring their 'beingness'.

7. Paradox

Previous leadership tuition had emphasised the need to find an answer to every question, because leaders had a need to be right.

This new approach recommended 'standing in the question' so that many possible answers can be considered. This requires an openess and a recognition that there is more than one right answer to any problem.

Females, with their increased connections and ability to hold more ideas within their heads at one time, find it easier to live with the concept of paradox.

8. Choice

A decision means resolving to take a course of action for a reason or a number of reasons. A decision has a big 'because' inside it, or a number of smaller 'becauses'.

A choice, on the other hand, is instinctive; it is made without reason. I just instinctively know after due consideration that this is the right course of action. I feel that it is right, but I can't guarantee it will produce the required result. The Eskimo instinctively feels when to wear skis as opposed to snowshoes. 'On the pitch', the gifted athlete instinctively feels when to release the ball and how much weight to put behind it. It is not a decision; it is a choice.

Choices are unconditional. An individual can unconditionally choose to live the life of his or her choice. It is not a decision, made for a reason. It just feels intuitively right. This non-linear thinking involves making a choice about who you want to be, making decisions about what you want to do and then about what you need to know.

Females, with their greater appreciation of paradox and ability to think of many things at the same time, found this concept of choice far easier to grasp. In contrast, males find it easier to understand the more logical concept of decision.

Here are some of the introductory notes to a transformational leadership programme from 1995. They have a definite feminine ring to them:

'This forum provides a breakthrough in the technology of living powerfully, living effectively, living an extraordinary life. It is a penetrating, challenging and practical inquiry into the issues at the heart of our lives – communication, relationship, happiness and satisfaction. It is about creating an opening for new thinking which allows for non-linear results.'

Here are the objectives of another of the same period:

- *Acquire new non-linear ways of thinking and dealing with the future.*
- *Access deeper levels of personal commitment.*
- *Learn and use a new, more effective language at work.*
- *Redefine relationships to increase productivity and creativity.*
- *Create a climate of openness and honesty.*
- *Learn to listen in a new way.*

Even though men led these programmes, the message coming across was *'learn to think in a female way'*. These were men trying to teach other men how to think like females. For women, seminars such as these were statements of the obvious, once the complications of the science, psychology and philosophy were stripped away. Females often wonder why the men struggle to grasp these concepts.

Here are Brian's comments after attending a seminar in 1994:

'As a director of a firm of insurance brokers with responsibilities for staff, turnover and profit, I certainly found the ideas mystifying the first time I heard them. They were just theories to me. And it was all embedded in metaphysics, new biology, eastern religion, philosophy and psychology, about which I knew little and had not got the time to learn. The logic was difficult to follow.

'There was no quick fix. There was no structure; there weren't enough models and checklists. There was no hard evidence that if I did change my behaviours, bottom-line benefits would occur at work. There was no suggested action; they did not advise me what to do. The male programme leader said I had to make a choice, but a choice about what?

'Developing a relationship, just to develop a relationship, was a foreign language to me. I telephoned people if I wanted something doing; I held a conversation to cause something to happen, not for the sake of conversation itself. I couldn't run a workplace like a dinner party! Nothing would ever happen if we operated like this and the competition in my industry was becoming more ruthless by the day. My competitors were doing things and unless I took action quickly, my company would be going out of business.

'One of the themes expressed was that I didn't need to be right. I thought that I was paid to be right – to make the right business decisions. I had responsibilities to shareholders and to other stakeholders to be right.

'Nevertheless, there was a nagging thought at the back of my mind that we needed to change the way we did things at work. We needed a breakthrough, because current working practices were not producing the same results they had in the past. So I started to read the reference list we had been given. I started to write my thoughts down. The process took nine months before I realised the impact that this new way of transformational thinking could have.'

This was no quick-fix leadership solution for Brian. It took time and considerable effort and did not come easily. His brain had to be completely rewired and that was hard work. This way of thinking did not sit naturally with his typically male brain. His advice to males is to be prepared to work at this stuff, because it isn't easy. He equates it to running uphill.

There are some male writers, gurus, lecturers and coaches who have assumed that the only way to lead was to adopt female characteristics and feminine leadership models. In other words, to adopt a paradigm that 'the future is female'. For some males this idea was threatening. No man, proud of being male, wants to be seen as feminine. As Brian has bravely said during one of our many telephone conversations, *'I've spent the last five years working with these female paradigm models and only a few months ago, I came by the insight that I had spent that time learning to think like a woman.'*

We stress that we do not wish to be critical of the shift towards more feminine thinking within the leadership debate. It provides valuable insights into the concepts of leadership and personal development. Our only criticism of this approach is that it does not sit easily with the average male brain. Male leaders, in general, find it hard to relate to.

We would summarise the feminine leadership paradigm of the time as:

The feminine leadership paradigm

- Right brain.
- Derived from biology.
- Distinction based.
- Relationship orientated.
- Values driven.
- Non-linear thinking.
- Ontological.
- Leading from behind.

In a nutshell, the leader of the 1990s was a right-brained, female biologist thinking in a non-linear way about ontological methodologies. They concentrated on making distinctions, leading from behind and making choices not decisions. Here is our representation of the feminine leadership paradigm:

Feminine leadership paradigm

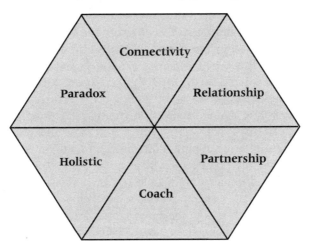

Again, we draw a parallel between the feminine leadership paradigm and physics. If you want to understand physics, you have to understand Newton's law of gravity, even though it has been surpassed by Einstein's thinking. In the same way, we recommend that if you want to understand the concept of leadership, you need to understand the feminine approaches taken in the 1990s.

Men, in particular, need to know how the female brain works, with its emphasis on relationships rather than action.

Learning from both approaches

The models and ideas we have explored, in themselves, are not masculine or feminine – they have taken on those characteristics through the way that they have been developed, and in their application in the workplace.

Leadership style of the 1970s and 1980s was not totally masculine. However, most learning focused on achieving the task.

It was a practical action-centred approach that sat comfortably in hierarchical organisations with clear chains of command.

Leadership style of the 1990s was not totally feminine. However, the focus was predominantly about developing relationships. It was an approach that sat more comfortably in realigned organisations with the flatter, team-based structures and more complex networks.

It is also worth noting that this different and feminine approach has penetrated leadership training courses and practice in some organisations. However, for many male leaders and organisations, these theories have made little impact. There are still many organisations that operate as controlling bodies, where resistance to change is strong and where women still have to adopt male thinking patterns.

We believe that identifying masculine and feminine leadership paradigms readily reveals how insensitively organisations have treated us as individuals, as human beings. It shows us that we need to engage people at work in ways that allow them to 'be' themselves as human beings first, and male and female second. The category is singular (human beings), not dual (women and men).

The challenge of leadership tomorrow

As we have stated before, we believe that the challenge for tomorrow's leaders is not to produce what is there already, nor is it to produce what would have happened anyway. The challenge is to recognise what is missing and then to invent a product, a service, or a combination of the two, to fill the identified gap.

In tomorrow's competitive climate we need everyone to be a leader at whatever level he or she occupies in an organisation. From manager to receptionist, from van driver to chief executive, from accounts clerk to director, we need everyone to show initiative. And this is irrespective of their gender. We need this initiative because we envisage the twin factors of speed and connectivity dominating our lives at work tomorrow.

Speed

Every aspect of business and life now takes place and changes in real time. News has always travelled fast. Now it seemingly travels instantaneously. Every televised news programme has reporters featuring items as they happen from the place where the news is occurring.

Newspaper proprietors realise that the teenage generation, the future purchasers, will not read papers for news. The young teenagers rely on TV or the Internet for news. Waiting for tomorrow to read the news is not good enough today. Consequently, newspapers have become much more about feature articles and comment.

There has been a dramatic drop in the time between ordering a product and receiving it. In 1997 Brian ordered his lap-top computer and received it custom-configured five days later from Dublin. Today, this five-day gap has shrunk to 72 hours, and in 2004 is likely to be same-day delivery. In Tokyo, you can order your customised Toyota on Monday and be driving it by Friday.

Speed is shortening product life cycles from years to months and in some cases even to weeks. The worldwide electronic network transfers money from one financial institution to another at the rate of $40 billion dollars a minute. For the individual, a day away from the workplace means scores of Email messages that have to be read and answered.

This predilection for speed is altering people's expectations. Customers now expect real-time responsiveness 24 hours a day, every day of the year. There is now a real premium attached to speed in business.

Connectedness

Mobile phones, pagers, personal computers, voice-mail systems, bar-code scanners, global positioning satellites, Email, the Internet and all of the other gadgets that connect us together are just the visible part of the connectivity story. Once all these systems connect up with each other, their actions will become unpredictable and will change the way the economies, businesses and individuals behave.

In the language of the science of physics this connectedness will produce a complex adaptive system. The human body is one such system. Each cell in the human body undertakes a particular function. For example, the body produces a completely new skin once a month. Most of the dust in the average house is human skin. Each cell in the body seems to know what to do and is in perfect relationship with every other cell. Each cell is both an independent system and reacts to stimuli for the benefit of the whole body.

We are now creating a vast system of worldwide connectedness through which information flows in real time. Computers are not now merely used for data crunching; they are used for connecting: people to people, machine to machine, product to service, network to network, organisation to organisation, and all the combinations thereof. We have created a complex adaptive system. And this system has a life of its own.

For the first time we have information flows that are owned by no one person or organisation. There is no chief executive in charge of, and accountable for, the performance of the Internet. It is growing of its own accord and making the rules up as it goes. We cannot predict the effects of all of this interconnectedness. We have to reach for the latest thinking in quantum physics, fuzzy logic and new biology to get even a sniff of understanding of how this system will react and develop.

In summary, speed and connectivity will dominate our lives at work in the next five years and these factors will necessitate the utilisation of the genetic strengths of both sexes. The necessary predilection for speed and action is essentially masculine, while the necessary preference for connectivity and relationships is essentially feminine.

Therefore, as we stated in the first chapter, our definition of leadership for the future is a combination of the more feminine paradigm:

'A reciprocal relationship between those who choose to lead, and those who decide to follow.'

KOUZES AND POSNER

And the more masculine paradigm:

'Leadership is achieving results through others'.

GARNETT

Putting the two together, our definition becomes:

'Building a reciprocal relationship between those who choose to lead and those who decide to follow, in order to achieve an agreed common purpose.'

We believe that leadership is not bestowed from above but granted through the trust of others. Anyone can choose to pick up the mantle and perform on the leadership stage. It was Shakespeare who said, *'All the world's a stage, and the men and women merely players'*. The problem with leadership is that once we choose to take up the mantle, we must step upon a stage.

As leaders, we have to choose what character we want to play on the stage. The fundamental problem for leaders is that often people think they have to be different from how they naturally are. We believe that we need to better understand the different ways that women and men choose to lead and decide to follow. And further, once we have understood the differences, we need to value the gifts that each sex brings to the leadership stage.

We seem to have moved through the following cycle:

- Post-Second World War, females had no choice but to adopt masculine characteristics if they wanted to perform on the leadership stage.
- And then, in the 1990s, the pendulum swung to the other extreme and males, in the opinions of some male writers and lecturers, had no choice but to adopt feminine characteristics if they wanted to perform on the same stage.
- We are now entering a third era, in which we need the strengths of both sexes to survive and prosper on the leadership stage.

Throughout the million years of our evolutionary past, right up to the emergence of the agrarian economies, males and females were of equal social importance. They depended upon one another in a social partnership that demanded equality. We need once again to return to this equality. We need to be equal *and* different. As a woman at work, Liz is conscious that so long as men hold the 'powerhouse' of the majority of the leadership positions, this may remain an ideal. As a first step, organisations must learn to value the strengths both sexes bring and reward them equally.

It is our belief that both men and women can become first-class leaders by recognising that each brings different strengths to the leadership party. Nature teaches us that those who can adapt to change will survive. Oak trees that are rigid in their past beliefs will be uprooted in the hurricane of change. Willows that can bend with the wind will live, grow and develop. Those male and female leaders who can adapt and bend will prosper.

Males and females can work side by side in a balanced relationship based on talent and skill, rather than gender, with the battle of the sexes relegated firmly to history. We can do this if we continue to increase our understanding of the different ways that each sex thinks and acts.

It is not a question of either/or; we will need both to succeed as leaders in the future. We need the strengths of both sexes to counteract the weaknesses of each sex. It is not a fight; it is a co-operative. Neither need emulate the other to succeed as leaders, both can be themselves. It is about leveraging diversity. We need leaders who don't talk as a man or a woman but engage as a person.

It is the job of the leader to unfreeze the stereotypical gender attitudes that have dominated our thinking on the equality issue, and get both sexes to recognise the strengths of each gender.

We believe that female- or male-loaded quotas are not the answer. We should deny no individual the career of their choice, but we must expect that males and females will choose different careers, because their brains are wired differently. Quotas will not make women, in general, want to become engineers, or men, in general, want to become nurses.

Females need to understand that it is natural for males to want to compete to lead. It is built into their brain chemistry. Men will naturally compete, and women need to recognise that this is a genetic response. Men will want to compete to be the best. Even in equality-driven Scandinavia, 90% of the top jobs are still held by men. Higher levels of testosterone mean that, on average, men have an edge in any competitive situation.

Males need to understand that the organisations of the future will have far more female characteristics than in the past. These organisations will be value-centred and show a caring for the community, both local and global. They will learn by experimenting and have partners rather than competitors. Rather than be driven solely by growth, they will have a much more holistic approach to business in the context of life now and in the future.

As leaders, we need to nurture and strengthen our connections in all areas – 'leadership' is latent within us all. Men will need to learn the techniques of dialogue and authentic listening. Women will need to learn the need for more urgent action and the necessity of taking more risks. The rest of the world will not wait in these times for every 'I' to be dotted and every 'T' discussed before any action takes place.

Men need to learn from women how to foster and develop relationships. Females need to understand that men do not share their predilection for discussion in groups. Men will need to become better at coaching, creating the space for others to show up in rather than being the captain on the field.

Women leaders need to understand that men require a structure that enables them to compete. Male leaders need to understand that females require an organisation that is far more value-centred.

Satisfying both needs is not impossible. This is one of the paradoxes of leadership that we predict will come to the fore in the next five years. Males need to learn an appreciation of paradox – that there will not be only one right answer to leadership dilemmas in this brave new world.

Our vision of leadership

The model we present here is not designed to reinforce gender stereotyping, but starts from where our individual strengths lie in nature. It allows each of us to retain our own identity. We believe that it encourages the best of both sexes and provides individuals with exposure to new situations and opportunities to learn and advance.

References

Adair, J., *The Action Centred Leader*, The Industrial Society, 1988.

Bennis, W. & Goldsmith, J., *Learning to Lead*, Nicholas Brealey, 1997.

Briley, S., ed., *Women in the Workforce*, HMSO, 1996.

Buzan, A., *Use Your Head*, BBC, 1974.

Conran, S., *Down with Superwoman*, Sidgwick & Jackson, 1990.

Covey, S., *The Seven Habits of Highly Effective People*, Simon & Schuster, 1992.

Covey, S., *Managing from the Left, Leading from the Right*, Simon & Schuster, 1996.

Davis, S. & Meyer, C., *Blur*, Capstone, 1998.

Garnett, J., *The Work Challenge*, The Industrial Society, 1974.

Goleman, D., *Emotional Intelligence*, Bloomsbury, 1996.

Klausur, *The Industrial Society*, publicity material, 1995.

Kouzes, J. & Posner, B., *The Leadership Challenge*, Jossey-Bass Publishers, California, 1995.

Landmark Forum, publicity material, 1995.

Mailer, C., Musgrave, P. & Desmons, G., *The History of The Industrial Society*, The Industrial Society, 1986.

Moir, A. & W., *Why Men Don't Iron*, Channel 4, HarperCollins, 1998.

Morris, D., *The Human Sexes*, Network Books, 1998.

Mulgan, G., *Connexity*, Chatto & Windus, 1997.

Senge, P., *The Fifth Discipline*, Century, 1990.

Trew, K. & Kremer, J., *Gender & Psychology*, Arnold, 1998.

Wheatley, M., *Leadership and the New Sciences*, Berrett-Koehler Publishers, 1994.

8

The marriage of two minds

'Everything you see and touch was once an invisible idea until someone chose to bring it into being. Any powerful idea is absolutely fascinating and absolutely useless until we choose to use it'

RICHARD BACH

We need leaders who can engage others as people not as men or women. We need leaders who can think as others do and connect with minds other than their own. We offer you a new leadership paradigm that honours the scientifically proven genetic strengths of both sexes.

We have taken our representation of the male and female leadership paradigms from chapter 7 and merged them into one model as pairs of leadership traits.

Mainly MALE Traditional 'Old leadership'	Mainly FEMALE Modern 'New leadership'
1. Action	1. Connectivity
2. Task	2. Relationship
3. Fragmentation	3. Holistic
4. Competition	4. Partnership
5. Risk-taking	5. Paradox
6. Captain	6. Coach

Traditionally the left-hand column would have been considered masculine, or more recently 'old' leadership; and the right-hand column feminine or 'new leadership'. We advocate that the leader of the future will need to develop all of these distinctions, travelling between each pair of leadership traits as the situation demands. It is not a question of either one or the other; both are needed for complete leadership.

A complete leadership model

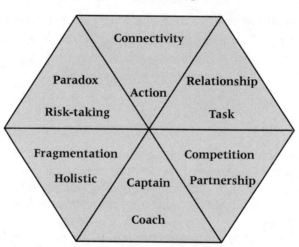

This is a complete leadership learning methodology. In this chapter we break down the leadership balance into its six constituent parts and offer a commentary on each one. We also apply the genetic strengths of each sex to the leadership distinction named.

In each pair of traits leaders need both sets of distinctions. It is not a question of either one or the other; both are needed for complete leadership. A distinction is a way of organising what we see. It is created in language and allows for possibility. The more distinctions we have available, the greater the possibilities we can create.

When you're four years old you have no distinction of 'cycling balance'. Only when you distinguish balance does it give you access to the whole idea of riding a bike, and all that that opens up to you. Your little world increases tenfold just by distinguishing cycling balance.

There are not many yellow Volkswagens. Liz knows this because she drives an atlantic blue one and she notices other Volkswagens on the road. However, if you suspect that your partner is having an affair with someone who drives a yellow Volkswagen, you will start to notice these cars everywhere. This is because you are really distinguishing yellow Volkswagens. What is scarce has become common because you are distinguishing powerfully.

This, however, is not a quick-fix solution. You have to work at making distinctions. You cannot become a cricket buff, a wine connoisseur or a music lover overnight. Neither can you become a complete leader immediately. When you are four years of age you have to work hard at distinguishing balance on a bicycle. In adulthood you even have to work at spotting yellow Volkswagens.

Segments of the leadership world

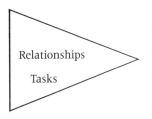

'Integrity and trustworthiness are the basis of every relationship' (Anon)

'Set the task of the team; put it across with enthusiasm and remind people of it often' (The Industrial Society, ACL card *c.*1973)

Both an emphasis on tasks and an emphasis on relationships are important. We need both to succeed as leaders.

Task orientation

In most organisations, we divide ourselves up into discrete units and organise ourselves along specific job lines, as Henry Ford and his production line taught us to do. We pay attention to our tasks, the jobs we have been allocated and the standards that we are asked to achieve.

And these are vitally important. Eddie Stobart runs an express haulage firm of more than 700 vehicles. He sets demandingly high standards for the tasks he asks his staff to perform. He sets standards of dress, of courtesy to other road users, of sticking to the law, especially speed limits, of courtesy to customers, of time-keeping and of delivery. The tasks and the standards are exacting and clearly communicated.

You might think that he would have difficulty recruiting drivers, but quite the reverse is true. His company is known as the company to drive for. He has a waiting list of potential applicants that is estimated to be five years long. Eddie knows the secret of setting the highest standards. He knows that these standards make a difference, a vital difference. His firm is exceptionally good at doing the tasks they promise their customers. He knows that his staff can be motivated by the sense of achievement.

At work a structure is used to make tasks easier to achieve. A school or a university would not be able to function without some division into departments. This division enables those with common interests to communicate more readily about the things that are important to the maths faculty or to the French department.

The work team must be small enough for this essential communication to take place. It is no accident that the largest team in sport consists of only 15 people on the rugby union field. Treating people as individuals, consultation and agreement of targets are all good reasons for keeping the work team small.

But structure is not the be-all and end-all of an organisation. The organisation exists to achieve a purpose. The purpose of a school is to provide the best all-round education and pastoral care for its pupils. This implies that there are processes to ensure that everything functions smoothly. For example, there needs to be a process that requires individuals and teams to communicate and co-operate across and outside structural boundaries. There needs to be a process by which communication is first established, then functions efficiently and finally acts as a learning mechanism.

Task orientation requires the male gifts of:

- target orientation
- focus
- structure and form
- action orientation.

And the female gift of:

- multi-tasking.

Relationship orientation

An entirely different approach is that of concentrating on relationships. From the holistic approach of quantum physics and the biological theory of complex adaptive systems, we know that reality is essentially defined by relationships.

The human body is one such complex adaptive system. Each cell in the body is in communication with every other cell. Each cell seems to know its own duty. The more each cell is in communication with the whole organism, the more it is able to fulfil its own task and consequently serve the whole system. As in the human body, every individual depends on and is affected by the work, ideas and actions of other individuals. Every one of us performs our work in a tightly woven, interactive and interconnected web of interdependent parts.

To meet current challenges in times of great change, we must explore the building of environments that support the development of relationships. We need to focus on how we can best get our work done together. We have much to learn from a team of ants that constantly shifts their individual positions to move a large object together. They seem to have a relationship that involves constant communication.

As human beings, what we can say to others, and what we can ask for from others, is limited to that which is allowed by the relationship between us. This can only be improved by having a conversation. When someone speaks to us we need to pay attention and really listen to them. We need to stop what we are doing, look at them and paraphrase their words to communicate our understanding of their words back to them. We don't just need to listen – we need to be seen to listen.

The most important thing that we can give to a relationship is time. We need to focus on the positive, and do things to make the other party feel special. We need to understand that we should never underestimate the value of an encouraging word. It may not mean much to us and we may have forgotten making it within half an hour. However, the warm feeling that we leave behind will remain with the recipient for a long time.

We need to avoid destructive criticism and sarcasm at all costs. If we need to criticise, we should criticise behaviour, not character, being hard on the issues but soft on the people.

Focusing on tasks is important, but so is that of developing relationships.

Relationship orientation requires the female gifts of:

- relationship orientation
- dialogue
- listening
- interpersonal connections
- social awareness.

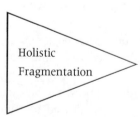

Holistic
Fragmentation

'The universe is a living, creative, experimenting experience of discovering what's possible at all levels of scale from microbe to cosmos' (Margaret Wheatley and Myron Kellner-Rogers)

'Everything should be made as simple as possible but not simpler' (Albert Einstein)

We all get stuck! We all have mechanisms that keep us where we are. For men it's about process and linearity. For women it's about not wanting to 'rock' relationships, of being unloved if we change something and someone doesn't like it. As leaders we need the ability to break things down into their component parts and to retain a holistic view of our world and the consequences that our actions mean for others.

Fragmentation

Each culture has its own fragmented way of looking at the world. In the west, this derives from the discoveries of Sir Isaac Newton, some 300 years ago. He gave us the way we think about the world today. He was the physicist who discovered the law of gravity. His thinking encouraged more scientists to strive to explain the previously inexplicable.

From a very early age we are taught to break problems apart, to fragment the world. If something isn't working we are taught to analyse where the problem is, seek the cause and then to fix it. We can then replace the problem employee, restructure a job assignment or re-divide a company into a new structure, just as we replaced the broken part of a toy when we were children.

Newton's discoveries made the results of the machine age possible. Essentially this way of thinking regards the universe as mechanistic, and assumes that everything consists of calculable individual components. We have a natural and valuable need to find out how things work and to discover why they don't work. And part of this we think of as logic.

Logic is defined as the science of pure reasoning. People often think that there is something cold about logic. Logic reminds us of Mr Spock, in *Star Trek*, playing multi-dimensional chess, his Vulcan brain remorselessly analysing every possible permutation before making a move. To the typical male brain, there is something extremely satisfying in being able to take a knotty problem and, having carefully unpicked the complications, arriving at the solution. It is an essential skill in business.

Females sometimes find this more difficult – with their wide-angle vision lens they tend to see things from many perspectives. How many times has a male told a female, *'But that's just not logical!'*? **Fragmentation** embraces the male gifts of:

- action orientation
- target orientation
- focus
- structure and form.

Holistic

For many simpler problems that face us at work, fragmentation and logic are often the best approaches to take. For more complex problems, however, we can pay a hidden and enormous price by taking this fragmented view. The mechanistic image of the world is deeply embedded in most of us, particularly men. And because of this, we can lose sight of the landscape of the consequences of our actions; we can lose our intrinsic sense of connection to a larger whole.

Based on new thinking from science, psychology and philosophy, a different paradigm has developed – the world is simply one whole. The world is a complex adaptive system and each cell has an effect on each and every other cell. For complex problems, solutions are to be found in the context of the whole, and in the individual parts. We need the big picture and the detail.

As leaders we need to develop the ability to hover above the forest and see the big picture below us. We need to be able to distinguish the wood from the trees and the trees from the wood. We need to understand the detail of the interconnections of the root structure that makes every tree stand both for itself and for every other tree. We need to understand that the twig is both an independent cell and an integral part of the branch, the branch an integral part of the tree and the tree an integral part of the forest.

In many companies the individuals have concern only for themselves, or their section, and not for the organisation as a whole. Leaders need to recognise that their ship, or their part of the ship, is part of the flotilla. The actions of one individual impact on the relationship that the company has with a client, and unless that individual is aware of the totality of the relationship, there is potential for damage.

An important part of the holistic leadership approach is that of constructing a vision that will motivate others. Visions are about beliefs and values that can allow others to align themselves and see that they can be part of a better future. It is the vision that gives hope and inspires.

Visions do not usually occur in blinding flashes of the obvious; they have to be worked at. They have to be teased down the stairs, one step at a time. Visions are not business plans. A business plan does not talk about hope. A plan has no vision, and it is the vision that inspires. A vision must be a dream in the Martin Luther King sense. It must be short, succinct, memorable and inspiring.

A Holistic approach requires the female gifts of:

- relationship orientation
- listening
- appreciation of paradox
- social awareness
- group working
- appreciation of distinction.

And the male gifts of:
- vision
- inventiveness
- risk-taking.

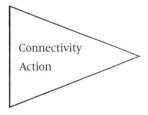

'*A connection is as real an ingredient in business as raw material, labour or finance – but it only exists when you can see it*' (Edward de Bono)

'*Just Do It*' (Nike advertisement)

Action

The average male brain is orientated to action. Through doing, the leader becomes. The need to accomplish the tasks for which the team, unit, department and, indeed, the organisation exists is a primary and obvious duty of any leader. A leader who consistently fails to achieve targets and budgets is unlikely to remain a leader for very long. However, we recognise and accept that never to fail is probably never to take a risk. Leadership is about having the courage to take action when the output of that action is not necessarily certain.

This makes it vital to achieve clarity of goal and objective, and an action orientation is a leadership approach that encourages the building of models, the listing of priorities and checking whether these tasks have been done. Leadership is therefore about taking action. This embraces not only the things that need to be done to achieve the task but also the actions necessary to support individuals and build teams.

This is about linearity and focus, for which the male brain with its sequential learning activities is more suited. When in action, and when doing, it is more difficult to see the big picture. With the speed of exponential change in the working environment today, an action-orientated approach can limit our ability to gauge the effect of our actions as leaders in the wider world.

Action requires the male gifts of:

- action orientation
- focus
- risk-taking.

Connectivity

Connectivity recognises that for every action there are several reactions and many of these will not be immediately self-evident to the action-taker. This approach recognises that everything in the universe is a complex adaptive system – a butterfly flapping its wings in the skies over Brazil can trigger a hurricane in Texas.

It is a concept that embodies a focus on relationships – people to people, object to object and information flow to information flow. A leader needs a recognition that what you are is more important than what you do. It is also about viewing fragments and connecting these pieces together to produce a methodology that can be applied to make a difference. A leader needs a wide-angle lens to appreciate the connectivity of his or her actions.

This approach recognises that, because inter-connectivity exists, there is often more than one right answer to any leadership situation. The ability to allow alternative actions to appear can be beneficial in the longer term.

Connectivity requires the female gifts of:

- relationship orientation
- dialogue
- listening
- paradox
- distinction appreciation.

And the male gift of:

- vision.

'*Good business should contain something for both parties*' (John Harvey Jones)

'*There are no prizes for coming second*' (Anon)

Competition

This leadership facet comes from the paradigm of 'I win: you lose'. This is the way we have been trained throughout our education. Examining boards only give a fixed percentage of 'A' grades. Therefore, if you get an 'A' grade, you win, but someone else with a 'B' grade has lost. The person with a 'B' grade has forced someone else down to a 'C' grade, and they in turn have forced another down to a 'D'. This is the basis of academic success.

On the sports field and in the arts we are taught to compete. There is the winning sports team and the winning choir, and there are those who did not win. We have lived with these patterns all of our lives. The judicial system is adversarial: if the defence wins, the prosecution loses. Democracy is adversarial. If the Labour Party wins the argument or the election, the other parties lose. Parliamentary debate is a competitive paradigm. It is the essence of democracy in the mother of all parliaments in Westminster. As a woman, it is a difficult place to be effective. Coote and Pattulo conclude that trying to adapt it to female needs is daunting and often discouraging.

The media portrays this competitive win/lose mentality every day. It is all around us. Every morning on Radio 4 a debate takes place with a skilled interviewer, such as John Humphrys, taking on a politician over the issue of the day. And at the end of the conversation it is always possible to judge who has won and who has lost.

The world of business is a competitive place. It is very necessary to compete externally. However, too often we carry these competitive attitudes into relationships inside our organisation. It is shown, for example, when the introduction of new computer systems requires the pooling of knowledge and contacts to enable everyone in an organisation to benefit from shared knowledge. The resistance from the average male brain will be extreme. In his eyes, he has spent years developing his own specialised knowledge and contacts, why should he give them away to others?

It is also evident when a lead for new business arrives and the recipient of the information decides to pursue the enquiry personally, rather than concede that the best approach may involve others handling the situation.

Competition has, at its heart, the male gifts of:

- competitiveness
- action orientation
- risk-taking

- status quo challenge
- desire to be the best.

Partnership

There are circumstances where we have to use the competitive win/lose paradigm. We can all use win/lose in sport. Not to do so would render the exercise almost pointless. There are situations in business where we are all forced to compete. However, conversations for a relationship have to be 'I win: you win' conversations. And win/win conversations are based on the concept of partnership.

Partnership relationships with others are based on equality. We can work towards a situation where relationships are based on 'I'm OK, You're OK'. We can work towards relationships where competition does not feature.

In contrast to competitive debate, partnership dialogue means finding the best way forward irrespective of who wins and who loses. It means seeing the whole amongst the parts and recognising the connections between the parts. It is enquiring into the assumptions and learning through disclosure. It means creating shared meaning amongst the participants. Dialogue implies a suspension of both judgement and the need for specific outcomes. It requires authentic listening and a slower pace, with an appreciation that silence is not threatening.

Partnerships require sharing and this is essentially a feminine characteristic. It stems from her predilection for intimacy rather than independence. Women like to talk, listen, discuss issues and get other people involved. They come up with answers through sharing their thoughts and feelings. Sharing can take time and it is considered important. Unless men have specifically asked for it, they tend not to want advice and prefer short, sharp conversations that get right to the action point. Sharing is not important to men; solutions are.

Some males may find this one hard. Driven by the desire to be the best, it is difficult for them to share where they are, or what they think about things.

The concept of **partnership** has, at its heart, the female gifts of:

- relationship
- dialogue
- listening
- coaching
- interpersonal connections
- multi-tasking
- appreciation of distinction.

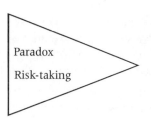

Paradox

Risk-taking

'Two men went to a court to settle a dispute. After the plaintiff had made his case, the judge said, "That's right". Then the defendant made his case and the judge said, "That's right". At this remark the clerk exclaimed, "They both can't be right". The judge replied, "That's right"' (Anon)

'And the trouble is, if you don't risk anything, you risk even more' (Erica Jong)

Business leaders are required to take risks sometimes in order just to survive. In some situations, therefore, the leader does have to be right. However, he or she does not have to be right all the time. Males, especially, need to recognise their own natural predilection for being right and to appreciate the necessity of the existence of paradox.

Risk-taking
The concept of risk is necessary in order for progress to happen. It is all about breaking loose from the constraints of the past and subjecting long-held beliefs to challenge. It is the process we go through to invent a future that is different from the past. The ability to define what may happen in the future and choose amongst alternatives lies at the heart of contemporary society.

We have risk-management techniques that can help us make a

vast range of decisions, from allocating wealth to safeguarding public health, from planning a family to waging war, from buying insurance to wearing seat belts, from planting potatoes to marketing cornflakes. We can minimise the risks, but fundamentally we have to take risks because the future is uncertain.

Business has always been about getting things right. In a world of constant and increasing change, there comes a time when we have to take a risk. A time when, even though we recognise that there may be many right answers, we have to back one horse in the business race.

The Newtonian world-view is that there is one right or best answer to our problems, and that it can be objectively determined. This idea was fundamental to the development of our experimental sciences. Researchers became objective observers of life around them and sought to discover how the world works definitively. We saw things as simply and entirely determined by cause and effect. Linear thinking is entirely cause and effect. It is non-animate. B should logically follow A, just as night naturally follows day.

Males may pride themselves on the ability to analyse data based on trends and simple curves. Accountants, economists and planners spend much time analysing the past and then planning for the future by extrapolating these curves. They take pride in choosing the right answer, betting on the right horse or making the right investment. And this is a very necessary function in business, but it is not the only way of looking at the world. Females may find risk-taking more difficult – with their wide-angle vision lens they tend to see things from many perspectives and therefore have more difficulty taking a risk.

Risk-taking involves the male gifts of:

- risk-taking
- inventiveness
- desire to be the best
- status quo challenge
- focus.

Paradox

There is security in the way we have always done things. It allows everyone to stay within his or her own comfort zones. It protects existing relationships and avoids risk. And this is a perfectly natural trait. For most work situations the way we have always done things can be effective. However, leaders are in the business of imagination – of thinking about the way things could be different.

We now understand from the quantum world-view that there are many right or best answers. Newton was convinced that light was a stream of particles emanating from a source in a straight line. The Dutch scientist Christian Huygens believed light to be in the form of a wave motion. This debate raged in the scientific community for three centuries before it was proved that both theories were 'right'. Light is both a particle and a wave.

Science tells us that there are no singular absolute and objective answers. It tells us that the observer influences the answer based on the expectations and assumptions that he or she brings to the process of observing.

When faced with difficult problems where complexity and paradox are present, it can be more useful to entertain many answers and experiment as we go along. In today's world, which is changing so quickly, it is often better to have a one-year budget and a flexible business plan than to adopt an inflexible five-year business plan.

Because the world today is moving very quickly, we need non-linear thinking that is based on connections from seemingly illogical parts of the universe. We need quantum leaps in thinking, productivity and action. These leaps can only come by holding on hard to the concept of paradox.

Paradox is fundamentally about the female gifts of:

- appreciation of paradox!
- listening
- dialogue
- appreciation of distinction.

As Liz has said many times, 'Most men just don't get this one!'

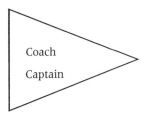

'*Coaching is not merely a technique to be wheeled out and rigidly applied in certain circumstances. It is a way of managing, a way of treating people, a way of thinking, a way of being*' (John Whitmore)

'*On the field the captain's job is to set the example in everything he does, however large, however small*' (Clive Lloyd)

Captain

The leader can often perceive himself or herself as the captain on the field, and this is a vital part of leadership. It is the captain's job to set the example by dint of the effort that they put into the job. It is their responsibility to motivate their team-mates by inspirational talks before the action.

There is a danger, however, that the captain assumes the leadership mantle in every work situation: chairs all the meetings, leads all the projects and the sales presentations. In so doing, she or he carries the weight of the total leadership for the whole of his or her organisation.

Fundamentally, captaincy is about making the decisions on the pitch in the workplace. Sometimes this is about top-down decision-making, and this can work well with power and control exercised at the top of the organisation. The flow of decisions emanates from the top and is disseminated to the staff below. Easy and efficient, this method can lead to rapid results in the short term. It also works well in a crisis.

Captaincy can be about a leader telling followers what to do. And sometimes this can make life easier for followers, so long as they agree with the top-down decisions that are made. It does, however, presuppose the leader's superior experience or wisdom, that she or he knows better than others do. Exercised continually, it can be disempowering to followers.

By nature, women find this more difficult. They want to talk things out, and this makes it hard for them to be the one to make the decision – independently.

The role of the leader captain can become one of acting as steward of the vision. This is done by 'walking the talk', by setting the example, by acting as a role model and constantly reminding the staff of the vision and purpose of their activities. The leader acting as a steward is protecting the organisation from itself in the same way that a steward at a football game is applying the rules and systems of crowd control to protect the crowd from itself.

Most organisations operate under a management-belief system called 'control', which is an essential part of the captain's make-up. The belief is that staff can't be trusted, so there is a need to install and operate systems that control staff. This belief has given us the hierarchies and pyramidal structures. It has given us profit centres, departmental boundaries and job descriptions.

Some control is necessary. Management is fundamentally about control. Leadership is about freedom, freedom for people to think for themselves. Leadership cannot exist without some management systems. Complete freedom is anarchy. A lack of control can lead to situations like Nick Leeson single-handedly bringing down Barings Bank.

Captains require the male gifts of:

- vision
- risk-taking
- target orientation
- desire to be the best
- focus.

Coach

An alternative paradigm is to view the job of the leader as a coach to encourage others to reveal their own true potential. The job of the leader is to create a future worth living. It is to get big commitments by making big requests of other people, and to give the necessary support so that people can fulfil their promise.

Another meaningful leadership model can then be added to the paradigm of captain on the field, involving the following leadership duties:

1. The formulation and communication of the vision and values.
2. The acceptance (or refusal with reasons) of the commitments coming from colleagues in a spirit of shared leadership.
3. Acting as coaches to their colleagues as they encourage the fulfilment of individuals' commitments.

This implies shared decision-making between leaders and followers. The logic is that if quantum leaps in productivity and creativity are needed, we must have the ideas and commitment of everybody in the organisation. This implies more of a shared identification with the problem and its solution.

Shared decision-making is recognisably slower. There is a real danger that a necessary decision will not get made at all. By nature men want to win and be in control, so shared decision-making is more difficult for them.

Work has become increasingly specialised and complex. This in turn creates increasing pressure on teamwork for desired results. Where we used only to develop individuals and self-mastery, we now need coaching for the development of whole teams. Integration of tasks and seeing how things fit together is key.

Most of us have been part of a 'great team' in business, in sport or some other activity. This great team probably had seven characteristics:

- The individuals trusted one another.
- They took the risks associated with earning trust from each other.
- The individuals were willing to learn from each other.
- They complemented each others' strengths.
- They compensated for each others' weaknesses.
- They had a common goal, purpose and approach.
- They produced extraordinary results.

They recognised their own diversity and played to it – and they usually had a very good coach and an excellent captain.

Coaching demands the female gifts of:

- coaching!
- relationship
- listening
- appreciation of distinction
- appreciation of paradox.

And the male gifts of:

- vision
- inventiveness
- focus.

Both males and females have gifts to bring to coaching. However, by nature, their styles can be quite different.

Applications of this model – the Leadership Mixing Deck

To be an effective leader in the future you will need to be able to adapt your behaviour to the situation in which you find yourself. Leaders have always had to do this, but in the future the need for agility and flexibility will increase, as demands on leaders grow to keep up with the exponential rate of change.

The leadership distinctions we have identified will need to be 'mixed', much as a recording technician 'mixes' sounds on the mixing deck in a studio. To create music you have different channels to represent the different sounds you are creating – piano, drums, singing, guitar, and so on. The technician decides how much of each channel is needed to get the sound that the artistes are looking for. He or she chooses how much or how little of each sound is required to get the best possible recording.

So in leadership, it is the job of the leader to decide how much or how little of each distinction is required in any situation, and lead accordingly.

Think of a crisis situation that has occurred because of external factors. Imagine that urgent action is required to protect the company's survival. Directive behaviours will be important, so my leadership mixing deck might look like this:

Action ....⊕.. Connectivity
Task ....⊕...................................... Relationship
Fragmentation ....⊕................................ Holistic
Competition.....⊕.................................... Partnership
Risk-taking ...⊕....................................... Paradox
Captain ...⊕.. Coach

If we now consider a longer-term research project, set up to look into new markets for our company, your mixing deck for the leader of that project would look very different:

Action ....⊕........ Connectivity
Task ....⊕.... Relationship
Fragmentation ....⊕......... Holistic
Competition............................⊕............. Partnership
Risk-taking ....⊕.................. Paradox
Captain ....⊕....... Coach

If we take yet another example, suppose our task now is the implementation of the launch of a new call centre for our company. All strategic decisions have been taken: the task is now one of implementation. The leadership mixing deck may look like this:

Action ....⊕...................... Connectivity
Task ....⊕.................... Relationship
Fragmentation ....⊕..................... Holistic
Competition...............................⊕........... Partnership
Risk-taking ....⊕................ Paradox
Captain ....⊕......................... Coach

So, by taking some common work experiences it is possible to see how the leadership balance can be brought to life. To think of every situation leaders might find themselves in would be unrealistic. Every situation will be unique and the components required for success different. It is the job of the leader to assess the situation and draw on the relevant leadership distinctions that comprise the leadership balance.

References

Bernstein, P. L., *Against the Gods*, John Wiley & Sons, 1998.

Coote, A. & Pattulo, P., *Power and Prejudice*, Weidenfeld & Nicolson, 1990.

Ellinor, L. & Gerard, G., *Dialogue*, John Wiley & Sons, 1998.

Garnett, J., *The Work Challenge*, The Industrial Society, 1974.

Harris, T., *I'm OK, You're OK*, Arrow, 1995.

Lorenz, E., *Predictability: Does the Flap of a Butterfly's Wings in Brazil Set Off a Tornado in Texas*, MIT Press, 1979.

Thomson, K., *Passion at Work*, Capstone, 1998.

9

The language of leadership

'You see it's like a portmanteau — there are two meanings packed into one word'

LEWIS CARROLL

As female and as male, we say one word and often it means something else to the other, as we have discovered, both to our individual cost and our mutual benefit. We therefore have to be clear what each of us means when we speak and to be able to listen and be aware of the differing male and female interpretations.

To Liz, relationships and dialogue are impossible without sharing. This involves finding out how others feel about situations and having the space in the conversation for her to say how she feels. Sharing takes place for the sake of sharing. She just knows that the sharing will be worthwhile. It demonstrates an underlying belief in synergistic relationships. Put two people who are willing to share together and they will always achieve more in harmony than they would have done independently.

Dr Joyce Brothers speculates that woman seems to feel that the proper study of woman is woman, and the more a woman knows about herself and others the better she will function. Not only that, but woman is willing to share her self-knowledge with the world.

In support of this conclusion she presents the evidence of sharing from women's magazines. Men's magazines, in contrast, give little insight into the way that men feel at significant times of their lives, like marriage or attending the birth of children.

To Brian, men like to provide solutions from their own knowledge, to give answers, show that they know what to do and then just do it. They have a focus on their own independence and action, which is entirely different from the female predilection for sharing. Whether it is captaining a football team or leading a workforce, men think action before communication. To many, the action is the communication.

Each sex starts the leadership journey from different places. Neither place is right or wrong. They are just different, and we need to recognise and value this difference.

What follows is what the language of the leadership model means to each of us, as a woman and a man. The following pages record our own spontaneous response to a word in the model. These responses confirmed again that we are very different.

Action

A feminine interpretation	A masculine interpretation
• It's getting on with things.	• It's about being able to see a longer-term vision that an action helps achieve.
• A conversation is action, probably the most important kind of action.	• It's the sheer joy of doing something well.
• Action is not only about doing things.	• It's a preference for doing rather than talking about doing.
• Beliefs and values surrounding the action have to fit with my own.	• It's not talking about things or feelings.
	• Action is both enjoyed during the doing and afterwards, thinking about a thing well done.

Brian describes the feeling when orienteering of being in tune with the map and the ground he is covering in the forest. At times, when things are going well, he can stand to one side and watch himself perform. Afterwards he takes great delight in analysing his performance and in telling others about it. This is a foreign language to Liz, to whom the beliefs and values are far more important than the action itself.

Connectivity

A feminine interpretation	A masculine interpretation
• The act of creation is the conversation.	• The act of making the connection forms the idea.
• You need relationships to make connections.	• The formation of the idea is creativity.
• Seeing things as they are, and being able to link them up unusually.	• From connections come inventions.
• Recognising that everything is connected – the process involved is seeing the connections – and that you see connections through conversation.	• It's something that happens inside my own head.

Connections for Liz come through other people; for Brian they happen in his own mind. Several female friends of ours have complained that they have never met a man who really tells them how they feel. The sharing of feelings about an issue is an important part of the connectivity process to Liz. Brian needs the space alone to work a problem through and make the connections in his own mind.

Paradox

A feminine interpretation	**A masculine interpretation**
• There are many different paradigms.	• This is an academic approach.
• It's OK for people's thinking to come from different places.	• Economists say 'on the one hand ... on the other hand ...' they can't make up their minds.
• It will work out all right you in the end – just give it time – things will become clear.	• There comes a time when have to make up your mind.
• There isn't an end anyway, because things will have moved on tomorrow.	• Appreciation of paradox is difficult, well nigh impossible.

This is best illustrated by the difference between closed thinking and open thinking. Closed thinking looks for the right answer to a problem. Open thinking looks for the right question. From the right question can come hundreds of possibilities for different solutions. It is then possible just to stand in the question and let the right solution become apparent. Standing in the question is not inaction, but it does require faith that the right answer will become apparent in time. Liz is much better at this type of open thinking than Brian. He looks for solutions rather than waiting for the answer to come to him over a period of time.

Risk-taking

A feminine interpretation	**A masculine interpretation**
• I would not walk willingly towards it.	• This is fun, a buzz.
• I'd rather not be in that place.	• It gets the adrenalin going.
• I will avoid it if I can.	• It's someone or something to compete against.

- I have to talk myself into it, and then I can do it.
- I have to believe it is possible.
- I feel good when I have done it.

- Of course, there isn't just one right answer. This is a very restricted view of the world.
- Risk can damage relationships.

- I feel good when I'm doing it, as well as afterwards.
- It's about action.
- It's thinking outside the box and challenging the status quo.
- There has to be one right answer in business, you can't back every horse in the race.
- There is only one winner; there are lots of losers.

It is interesting that Brian concentrates on action and Liz on belief. The word risk is derived from an Italian word *risicare*, which literally means 'to dare'. Risk-taking is about daring to do something; often others may think what you are attempting is impossible.

Pete Goss, the British round-the-world yachtsman who was awarded the legion of honour by the French government for his heroic rescue of a French competitor on Christmas Day in 1997 in the La Vendee race, puts it this way:

'It is not the critic who counts, or the man who points out where the doer of deeds could have done better. The credit belongs to the person who is actually in the arena, whose face is marred by dust and sweat and blood … their place shall never be with those cold and timid souls who know neither victory nor defeat.'

To Liz, risk is not about money or things; for her, people are the biggest risk to worry about. Her concern is that a risk may damage a relationship and that this could take time to repair or even prove irreparable. Brian is with Pete Goss on this one. In other words, sod the hesitant, the doubters and the critics, let's just get on with it.

Fragmentation

A feminine interpretation	**A masculine interpretation**
• It's boring examining bits of the whole. I need to see the big picture.	• You break things down to find out how they work.
• Why bother, it's about things, and people are more important.	• It's necessary for any kind of mass production or a task that has to be repeated.
• It doesn't matter how the phone or the video works so long as they do.	• It's fun taking things to pieces to find out how they work.

Liz's brother, Rob, is an engineer by profession. He excels at writing the technical detail of reports but always has difficulty phrasing the executive summary. Liz speculates that if she and her brother worked together, she could easily do the summaries and the overview from her holistic approach, deriving from a typically female brain, and relieve Rob's male brain of this pressure. Together, they would be better leaders than they are individually.

Holistic

A feminine interpretation	**A masculine interpretation**
• It's about 'well-being'.	• Big picture.
• Everything is connected to everything else in the universe.	• It's about seeing the forest and the trees.
• Everything matters. Nothing is more important than anything else.	• It's important to be able to see holistically in order to translate it into a vision.
• The whole person matters, not just bits of them.	
• Caring should embrace the concept of whole being.	

This is interesting, as Liz has put the holistic concept in terms of people and Brian has put it in terms of things. One of Liz's friends was badly injured in a car accident and was in hospital for many months. He was well served by numerous specialists, who took care of the repair to different parts of his body. However, his complaint was that no one doctor or carer was responsible for the well-being of the whole person.

Captain

A feminine interpretation	A masculine interpretation
• Gives direction.	• Plays on the pitch at the same time as the rest of the team.
• Decides tactics, but not strategy.	• Sets the example by dint of his or her own efforts.
	• Is in charge of team talks and these are meant to inspire greater effort.
	• Makes the key decisions on the field of play.
	• Takes individuals to one side for discipline or motivation.

The important role of the captain has been slipping in British industry for some time. Structures have been flattened and management layers removed. As we have drifted in leadership education towards empowerment and non-directive coaching, the role of the captain who says to his sales team, for example, 'Give me your three most difficult accounts and I will make a success of them' seems to have vanished. We believe that leaders have a significant role to play as captains on the pitch of life at work.

Coach

A feminine interpretation	A masculine interpretation
• Helps me to see my own potential.	• Does not play on the pitch at the same time as the rest of the team.

- Exposes the pieces of me that I cannot see myself.
- Supports, encourages and nurtures me.
- My own development will help others.

- Makes the key decisions off the field of play.
- Takes individuals to one side for discipline or motivation.
- I am my own coach.
- You should not need one, or only rarely in times of great difficulty.

To Liz, a non-directive coach helps her break down her own holistic approach into fragmented pieces or bite-sized chunks. Her coach helps her find a start point to a big issue and to see things that she might have missed. Brian has never used a non-directive coach. He prides himself on being able to sort out solutions to all of his own problems.

Competition

A feminine interpretation

- I am competitive if I am put in a competitive situation.
- I do not compete in conversation.
- Competition between ideas can be valuable but not between people.

A masculine interpretation

- I seek out competitive situations.
- I will walk away from non-competitive conversations.
- Competition makes me strive to be the best.
- It makes the world keep improving.
- There are no prizes for coming second.

Liz and Brian often lecture together, appearing on the same platform at the same time. Almost all public speakers are now evaluated by their audience. Brian eagerly awaits the arrival of the evaluation analysis, when he can compare his own evaluation to those of the other speakers. He even pins the best ones on his office wall. In contrast, Liz barely glances at them. And on some occasions she has even forgotten to open them.

When asked to define a debate, Liz concluded that it was a listening and sharing of ideas, a recognition of the views of others, and she reserved her right to change her mind and cross the debating floor. In contrast, Brian felt it was about cut and thrust, winning and losing, about not being proved wrong in public and about sticking to the rules of the debate.

Partnership

A feminine interpretation	A masculine interpretation
• Security from personal risk-taking.	• They are a necessity of life but I would rather not be involved.
• I can only be half-wrong, if there are two in the equation.	• People tend to let me down in partnership.
• A shared accountability is reassuring.	• Guilt is something I do not feel.
• I feel guilty if I let people down.	• I always do what I say I'm going to do; others do not.
• I need partnerships.	
• From equal effort you both derive equal gain.	
• Connections will flow from a partnership dialogue.	

A true partnership means that there is equal effort, equal potential for gain and equal potential for loss. Brian has lost a great deal of money in business partnerships that did not adhere to this principle. He now recognises that they were not true partnerships. Either the effort expected, the potential for gain or the potential for loss were not equal between the partners. Liz has more personal need for partnerships and is more willing to share.

Tasks

A feminine interpretation	A masculine interpretation
• Things that have to be done.	• Doing is being.
• Things to tick off lists.	• Pure joy in achievement.
• A bit of an inconvenience.	• To do: this is my life.
• Things that have to be completed before we can move on to developing relationships.	• It's 'being on the pitch'.
	• Challenging tasks provide satisfaction in themselves.

Liz has often been heard to say at work, 'Let's get the things we *have* to do or talk about out of the way, and then we can have a meaningful discussion about our relationship'. To Brian, the conversation stops when the things we have to do or achieve have been concluded.

Relationship

A feminine interpretation	A masculine interpretation
• The key to life.	• They have to be worked at.
• Essential for working together.	• They are hard work.
• It's about liking and being liked.	• You form relationships to get things done.
• Finding out how others feel.	• A necessary expenditure of time to guarantee achievement of a team task.
• Having the space to say how I feel.	

To Liz, life at work is about conversation and building relationships. It is literally all she does all day, every day. She has the responsibility for creating relationships with major clients as a corporate account manager. She remembers birthdays, and cards are sent to arrive on the right day. Personal thank-you notes are delivered promptly. Calls are made to develop a relationship, not for what she can gain from it. When a male business colleague went on secondment with his organisation to Switzerland for two years, he reported that only his female friends remained in touch with him.

References

Bernstein, P. L., *Against the Gods*, John Wiley & Sons, 1998.

Brothers, J. Dr, *What Every Woman Should Know About Men*, Granada, 1982.

Goss, P., *Close to the Wind*, Headline, 1998.

10

A vision of complete leadership

'To undertake a project, as the word's derivation indicates, means to cast an idea out ahead of oneself so that it gains an autonomy and is fulfilled not only by the efforts of its originator but, indeed, independently of them as well'

CZELAW MILOSZ

The spatial awareness of the average male brain finds the actions of drawing and reading a map relatively easy. This map fragments the beauty of the three-dimensional world around us into two physical dimensions. The map shows yet another different kind of beauty. Males can then rotate this map in their mind's eye, and they even read it upside down. The achievement of producing the map or the action of reading the map provides a sense of satisfaction that females find hard to understand. Males exist in a world of doing.

The more communicative average female brain does not see the world in two dimensions like this; they see the world as a three-dimensional hologram. It has a different beauty, not in the physical sense, but in all of the fascinating dimensions of conversation and relationships. These relationships and conversations exist for their own sake and have a three-dimensional beauty simply because of their existence. Females exist in a world of being.

Action is less important than conversation to the average female brain and achievement less important than relationships. And the reverse is true for the male. Conversation is less important than action to the average male brain and relationship less vital than the successful achievement of a challenge.

This book describes both aspects of the journey that we have taken: action and communication; spatial awareness and verbal fluency; doing and being. And our journey is by no means complete. We have, however, enjoyed it so far and learned much from each other along the way.

Neither of us could have produced this book alone. The result is a combined effort of one brain that was built to compete and another that was designed for partnership.

From a male perspective, and at the risk of embarrassing Liz, when we started this project, it was a mere idea formed over lunch. We didn't have a clue where to start. There seemed to be so many conflicting themes. This bothered Liz not at all. There was always another book to read, another piece of research to undertake, or someone else with whom to develop a relationship. Brian was just impatiently looking for the right answer. He found it frustrating that she could effortlessly and simultaneously hold opposing ideas in her head.

From a female point of view and at the risk of embarrassing Brian, if it were not for his gifts of translating ideas into vision this book would never have been written. Liz doesn't know quite how he does it. He is so focused. He has also brought the gift of risk-taking to this partnership. We have written this book in the form of a play and performed it in public many times. To Liz, that required a huge investment in risk-taking, a gift in which her typically female brain lacks connections.

The inferences we have drawn are a result of insights from the software of both minds that are in turn derived from the hardware of our different brains. Through working with each other, one male brain designed for action has learned the value of concentration on relationships and begun to grasp the importance of an appreciation of paradox. The other female brain built for communication has begun to see value in taking a risk and to appreciate the necessity of a laser-like focus to get things done to the deadlines we agreed.

Leadership in the future requires this unique combination. He needs to learn the feminine distinctions of leadership and she needs to learn the masculine distinctions. It is not either one or the other. Both are needed for future leadership effectiveness. We all need the masculine predilection for action and the female predilection for connectivity. We are equal and different. We can both learn from each other to develop the leadership distinctions that we do not possess to the necessary level. We can help each other to develop as leaders and as human beings.

To repeat our statement in the opening chapter, we stand for leaders engaging others as people – not as men or as women. We need leaders who can think as others do and connect with minds other than their own.

We hope that we have helped leaders make new and useful distinctions rather than snap judgements based on stereotypes. Our objective is to help both sexes to better understand work colleagues when their perceived behaviour differs from what one might expect.

Our aim is to show the paradox that exists in leadership within organisations. As with many issues, it is not a question of either/ or, right/wrong. It is about both existing in relationship with the other.

One last question, asked with our tongues only slightly in our cheeks. What could our organisations achieve if we employed joint chief executives – one male and one female, reflecting the full spectrum of the leadership gifts each sex brings to the equation?

And finally, as we said at the beginning of the book, we welcome readers' views, which will only add to our own knowledge, and the debate on the leadership implications of gender.

To contact the authors, please write, fax or Email to:

The Industrial Society
Campaign for Leadership
Robert Hyde House
48 Bryanston Square
London W1H 7LN

Fax: 44 171 723 2007
Email: Liz Cook c/o PHealey@indsoc.co.uk
Email: Brian.Rothwell@btinternet.com
Website: www.indsoc.o.uk

Appendix 1

The Liberating Leadership list of the 38 behaviours comprising good leadership

They are divided and sectioned to create the pneumonic L.E.A.D.E.R.

Leadership	Behaviours
Liberates	1. Does not blame people for mistakes.
	2. Encourages people closest to the job to make their own decisions.
	3. Listens to their staff.
	4. Encourages full and open communication.
	5. Operates systems based on trust, rather than suspicion.
	6. Encourages staff to develop new ideas.
Encourages	7. Accepts responsibility for the actions of their staff.
	8. Gives praise where it is due.
	9. Recognises and acts to minimise other people's stress.
	10. Supports staff when they need support.
	11. Regularly meets with individuals to clarify direction.
	12. Makes people feel important and shows that they have faith in them.
Achieves purpose	13. Achieves results.
	14. Agrees demanding targets with individuals and teams.

15. Consults those affected before making decisions.
16. Is willing to take unpopular decisions in order to move forward.
17. Seeks out future challenges and opportunities.
18. Regularly communicates an inspirational view of the future.
19. Constantly seeks to improve the way things are done.

Develops people and teams

20. Encourages others to learn.
21. Encourages others to work together as a team.
22. Regularly meets with the team to review progress.
23. Takes time out to guide and develop their staff.
24. Deals effectively with breaches in standards of behaviour.
25. Treats the mistakes of others as learning opportunities.

Example to others

26. Actively encourages feedback on their own performance.
27. Communicates an air of enthusiasm.
28. Works on their own learning.
29. Practises what they preach.
30. Openly admits mistakes.
31. Sets a good example by their own behaviour.

Relationships built on trust

32. Does not put self-interest before the interests of staff.
33. Keeps promises and does what they say they will do.

34. Is in touch with and sensitive to others' feelings.
35. Is calm in a crisis, and when under pressure.
36. Is honest and truthful.
37. Does not take credit for other people's work.
38. Is always fair.

Source
Turner, D., *Liberating Leadership*. The Industrial Society, 1998.

Appendix 2

Masculine and feminine organisational cultures

These different interpretations of the same leadership distinctions do not only apply to individuals; they can also apply to organisational cultures. Again we are not saying that one culture is right and another wrong; they are just different.

The ways of spotting male and female cultures in organisations:

Feminine cultures

- There is a focus on relationships rather than action. There are lots and lots of meetings, and the meetings are lengthy, often all-day affairs. The atmosphere is open and friendly. There are lots of people chatting in corridors and lifts. They are concerned about how people are feeling.
- There is also an infinite variety of different types of meetings. There are one-to-one meetings, team meetings, project meetings, learning network meetings, all-staff meetings and 'blue sky' meetings. Everyone is involved.
- There is usually a big team that makes the important decisions, and this team is willing to take time over the process, which is formulated.
- They have a published set of values and beliefs and try hard to live up to them. They have a holistic approach. There are discussions about the purpose and meaning of the organisation.
- There is a vision which is not necessarily materially based.
- There are lots of ideas and possibilities floating around. They understand the need for big changes.
- They can make connections with ideas from different industries.
- They understand the need for benchmarking.

- They compete less; rather they prefer partners and are willing to accept partnership rather than ownership.
- The pace of innovation and change is slower and more cautious. It is relatively difficult to get things to change or for action to happen. Consultation procedures are lengthy and care is taken to ensure that everyone has 'bought into' the proposed action. Sharing of ideas is big on the agenda. Dialogue rather than debate rules OK.
- They understand the concept of paradox and don't keep striving for one right answer.
- They are low on risk-taking but high on experimentation.
- They are big into learning as teams as well as individual development.
- The leadership is shared from project to project and leadership is not a function of status.
- There are relatively few captains on the field and many coaches attempting to improve the performance of others.
- The size of the phone bill is large.
- Thank-you notes and cards are in abundance. They are issued both to staff by staff and to customers and suppliers.
- The style of dress is individual; not many will be dressed in the same way. There is no corporate uniform.

Masculine cultures
- The atmosphere is buzzing and busy with action.
- They are concerned with profit and the bottom line or they are share-price driven. There is an emphasis on job descriptions and tasks and consequently on the results achieved. They ask what is the payback and what is the value for money before taking decisions.
- Structure is emphasised. Restructures take place regularly.
- Strong individuals, and small teams of strong individuals, run the business. They have real power. These captains take the lead at every meeting and are in charge of every function. Decision-making is rarely shared.
- Things are broken down into functions or geographically. There

is a profit-centre and cost-centre mentality and people compete internally. They spend a lot of resource in allocating costs from cost centres to profit centres, and there are lots of arguments about this concept. Accountants proliferate as a result.

- Performance league tables are on show illustrating the importance of internal competition.
- They study and analyse their external competitors a great deal, but, strangely, benchmark hardly at all.
- There is a vision but it often concerns share price or market share. Alternatively it is to be the best in their field.
- There is an emphasis on measuring the past, partly because accountants proliferate.
- Knowledge is power and is kept confidential. There are always some figures that are not openly released. Knowledge is not shared readily. They are not too concerned with people's feelings.
- Meetings are short and joshing or argumentative, and they are willing to take decisions based only on part of the evidence. Debate rules over dialogue most of the time. Emphasis is on winning the debate by superior presentation and by force of personality.
- They seek the one right answer and the quick-fix solution.
- They take big risks, banking on the fact that they have the one right answer. There is little tolerance of the likelihood of the existence of paradox.
- There is little emphasis on learning as a team but great stress is laid on individual qualifications and development.
- The phone bills are relatively low. Phone calls are short and swift, to the point.
- The dress code tends towards uniformity. People dress in similar ways.
- Salaries are competitive within the industry, certainly not below the norm. And this applies at the top of the organisation in spades!

Reference
Itzin, C., *The Gender Culture in Organisational Change*, Routledge, 1995.

References and bibliography

AA Foundation for Road Safety Research, University of Reading. *Male and Female Drivers – How Different Are They?* AA, 1998.

Adair, J., *The Action Centred Leader*, The Industrial Society, 1988.

Bennis, W. & Goldsmith, J., *Learning to Lead*, Nicholas Brealey, 1997.

Bernstein, P. L., *Against the Gods*, John Wiley & Sons, 1998.

Biddulph, S., *Manhood*, Hawthorn Press, 1998.

Briley, S., ed., *Women in the Workforce*, HMSO, 1996.

Bronowski, J., *The Ascent of Man*, BBC, 1973.

Brothers, J. Dr, *What Every Woman Should Know About Men*, Granada, 1982.

Buzan, A., *Use Your Head*, BBC, 1974.

Carnegie, D., *How to Win Friends and Influence People*, Ebury Press, 1998.

Carter, R., *Mapping the Mind*, Weidenfeld & Nicolson, 1998.

Channel 4 Television, three-part documentary, *Why Men Don't Iron*, broadcast summer 1998.

Conran, S., *Down with Superwoman*, Sidgwick & Jackson, 1990.

Coote, A. & Pattulo, P., *Power and Prejudice*, Weidenfeld & Nicolson, 1990.

Covey, S., *The Seven Habits of Highly Effective People*, Simon & Schuster, 1992.

Covey, S., *Managing from the Left, Leading from the Right*, Simon & Schuster, 1996.

Davidson, M. J. & Cooper, C. L., *Shattering the Glass Ceiling*, Paul Chapman Publishing, 1992.

Davis, S. & Meyer, C., *Blur*, Capstone, 1998.

de Bono, E., *Opportunities*, Pelican, 1980.

Driscoll, R., *The Stronger Sex*, Prima, 1998.

Durkin, K., *Developmental Social Psychology*, Blackwell, 1995.

Edley, N. & Wetherall, M., *Men in Perspective: Practice, Power and Identity*, Prentice Hall/Harvester Wheatsheaf, 1995.

Edvinson, L. & Malone, M., *Intellectual Capital*, Piatkus, 1997.

Ellinor, L. & Gerard, G., *Dialogue*, John Wiley & Sons, 1998.

Fielding, H., *Bridget Jones's Diary*, Picador, 1996.

Fromm, E., *To Have or to Be*, Abacus, 1979.

Garnett, J., *The Work Challenge*, The Industrial Society, 1974.

Gee, M., *The Ice People*, Richard Cohen Books, 1998.

Goleman, D., *Emotional Intelligence*, Bloomsbury, 1996.

Goodman, J., *Nature's Mind: The Biological Roots of Thinking, Emotions, Sexuality, Language and Intelligence*, Penguin, 1992.

Goss, P., *Close to the Wind*, Headline, 1998.

Gray, J., *Men Are from Mars, Women Are from Venus*, Thorsons, an imprint of HarperCollins, 1992.

Gray, J., *What Your Mother Couldn't Tell You and Your Father Didn't Know*, Vermillion, Ebury Press, 1994.

Gray, J., *Mars & Venus: A Match Made in Heaven?*, Newleaf, Gill & MacMillan, 1999.

Greenfield, S., *The Human Brain: A Guided Tour*, Phoenix, 1997.

Greer, G., *The Female Eunuch*, Paladin, 1970.

Gross, R., *Psychology: The Science of Mind and Behaviour*, Hodder & Stoughton, 1996.

Harris, T., *I'm OK, You're OK*, Arrow, 1995.

Hofstede, G., *Culture's Consequences*, Sage Publications, 1980.

Howells, K., *The Psychology of Sexual Diversity*, Blackwell, 1984.

Hyde, T. S. & Jenkins, J. J., 'Recall for words: a function of semantic, graphic & syntactic orienting tasks', *Journal of Verbal Learning and Behaviour*, 1973,12, 471-480.

Itzin, C., *The Gender Culture in Organisational Change*, Routledge, 1995.

Jones, S., *In the Blood: God, Genes and Destiny*, Flamingo, 1996.

Jost, A., 'Hormonal factors in the development of the male genital system', *The Human Testes*, New York, Plenum Press, 1970.

Kelly, K., *Out of Control: The New Biology of Machines*, Fourth Estate, 1994.

Klausur, The Industrial Society, publicity material 1995.

Kohlberg, L., 'A cognitive-developmental analysis of children's sex role concepts and attitudes', *The Development of Sex Differences*, E. E. Maccoby, Stanford University Press, 1966.

Kouzes, J. & Posner, B., *The Leadership Challenge*, Jossey-Bass Publishers, California, 1995.

Kroeger, O. & Thuesen, J. M., *Type Talk at Work*, Tilden Press, 1992.

Kuhn, D., Nash, S. C. & Brooker, J. A., 'Sex role concepts of two- and three-year olds', *Child Development*, 49, 445–51, 1978.

Landmark Forum., publicity material, 1995.

Lawrence, G., *People Types & Tiger Stripes*, Center of the Applications of Pysychological Type Inc., Gainsville, Florida, 1996.

Lawson, I., *Leaders for Tomorrow's Society*, The Industrial Society, 1999.

LeVay, S., *The Sexual Brain*, MIT Press, 1994.

Lorenz, E., *Predictability: Does the Flap of a Butterfly's Wings in Brazil Set Off a Tornado in Texas*, MIT Press, 1979.

Maccoby, E. E., *The Development of Sex Differences*, Tavistock, 1967.

Maccoby E. E. & Jacklin, C. N., *The Psychology of Sex Differences*, Stanford University Press, 1974.

Magee, B., *The Story of Philosophy*, Dorling Kindersley, 1998.

Mailer, C., Musgrave, P. & Desmons, G., *The History of The Industrial Society*, The Industrial Society, 1986.

Mapstone, E., *War of Words: Men and Women Arguing*, Vintage, 1999.

Maturana, H. & Varela, F., *The Tree of Knowledge: The Biological Roots of Human Understanding*, Boston, Shambhala, 1987.

McDonald, T., *Clive Lloyd. The Authorised Biography*, HarperCollins, 1995.

Moir, A. & W., *Why Men Don't Iron*, Channel 4, HarperCollins, 1998.

Moir, A. & Jessel, D., *Brainsex*, Mandarin, 1996.

Money, J. & Ehrhardt, A. A., *Man and Woman, Boy and Girl*, Johns Hopkins University Press, 1972.

Morris, D., *The Human Sexes*, Network Books, 1998.

Mulgan, G., *Connexity*, Chatto & Windus, 1997.

Myers, I. B., & Myers, P. B., *Gifts Differing*, Davies-Black Publishing, Palo Alto, California, 1995.

Nicholson J., *Men and Women: How Different Are They?* Oxford University Press, 1993.

Nystrand, A., *New Discoveries on Sex Differences in the Brain*, National Institute for Ageing, Bethesda, 1996.

Ornstein, R., *The Psychology of Consciousness*, Penguin, 1975.

Ozaniec, N., *Teach Yourself Meditation*, Hodder, 1997.

Pease, A. & B., *Why Men Don't Listen & Women Can't Read Maps*, PTI, 1999.

Pinney, R., *Vanishing Tribes*, Barker, 1968

Ridley, M., *The Origins of Virtue*, Penguin, 1997.

Ridley, M., *The Red Queen*, Penguin, 1994.

Rose, S., ed., *From Brains to Consciousness*, Penguin, 1998.

Rosener, J., 'Ways Women Lead', *Harvard Business Review*, November–December, 1990.

Rothschild, M., *Bionomics: The Inevitability of Capitalism*, New York, Henry Holt & Co., 1995.

Rowbotham, S., *Hidden from History: 300 Years of Women's Oppression and the Fight against it*, Pluto Press, 1973.

Runge effective leadership programme, The Industrial Society.

Russo, E. & Cove, D., *Genetic Engineering, Dreams & Nightmares*, Oxford University Press, 1998.

Senge, P., *The Fifth Discipline*, Century, 1990.

Sharpe, S., *Just Like a Girl*, Penguin, 1994.

Smith, J., *Different for Girls*, Vintage, 1998.

Steinem, G., *Outrageous Acts and Everyday Rebellions*, New York, Rinehart & Winston, 1983.

Tannen, D., *Talking from 9 to 5*, Virago Press, 1995.

Tannen, D., *You Just Don't Understand: Men & Women in Conversation*, Virago Press, 1992.

Thomson, K., *Passion at Work*, Capstone, 1998.

Trew, K. & Kremer, J., *Gender & Psychology*, Arnold, 1998.

Turner, D., *Liberating Leadership*, The Industrial Society, 1998.

van de Castle, R., *Our Dreaming Mind*, Aquarian Press, 1995.

Van der Meer, R. & Dudink, A., *The Brain Pack*, Van der Meer Publishing, a division of PHPC, 1997.

Varela, F., *The Embodied Mind: Cognitive Science and Human Experience*, MIT Press, Cambridge, Mass., 1991.

Wajcman, J., *Managing like a Man*, Polity, 1999.

Walleczek, M., *Klausur*, The Industrial Society.

Wheatley, M., *Leadership and the New Sciences*, Berrett-Koehler Publishers, 1994.

Wheatley, M. & Kellner-Rogers, M., *A Simpler Way*, Berrett-Koehler Publishers, 1996.

Whitmore, J., *Coaching for Performance*, Nicholas Brealey, 1996.

Wilbur,K., *A Brief History of Everything*, Newleaf, Gill & MacMillan, 1996.

Williams, J. E. & Best, D. L., 'Cross-cultural views of women and men', *Psychology & Culture*, ed. W. J. Lonner & R. S. Malplass, Boston, Alleyne & Bacon, 1994.

Wolf, N., *The Beauty Myth: How Images of Beauty Are Used against Women*, New York, William Morrow, 1991.